Praise for Diane Keyes and *This Sold House*

"Tops on my wish list for Diane Keyes' *This Sold House* is that it would have been published about a year sooner. My family spent over a year trying to sell a home. If I'd had this incredible expert's wisdom to call on, we might have saved ourselves money, time, and a fair amount of anxiety! Diane entertains and educates in this easy-to-read book. If you want to dive into the real estate pool, consider this book a life preserver!"

—Joan Steffend, host of HGTV's *Decorating Cents*

"After having our condo for sale for a year, we got *This Sold House* and followed Diane's advice. We spent around $100, borrowed a few items from friends and spent a week getting it ready. Although there were six other units for sale in our building—and lots of new construction around us—we sold our home after the first showing! We highly recommend taking Diane's advice. It sold our house, and we're sold on *This Sold House*!"

—Will Harpest, teacher and Chicago homeowner

"While nothing beats Diane in person, *This Sold House* is the next best thing. This wonderful book is a must-read for Realtors®, sellers, and even buyers. If you or someone you care about is contemplating selling, you need this book. This is an edge that sellers shouldn't be without."

—Sarah M. Richard, Realtor®

"You should grab this book, read it cover to cover, and implement all Diane Keyes' ideas, tips, and techniques. Unlike most such books, *This Sold House* is written for common folk with limited money and little time to make elaborate changes. After reading the Curb Appeal chapter, I found several ways to make my own home more appealing and create a better first impression. Darn good ideas make this book worth your reading time and no doubt will be the ticket to a quicker and more profitable sale."

—Connie Anderson, president, Armchair Interviews
www.ArmchairInterviews.com

"I love this book. Chock full of common sense, it is useful not only for sellers but also those looking to simplify and make their home more appealing to everyone. I refer to it often and will recommend this book to all my friends, whether they are planning to move or not. It is the perfect handbook to help homeowners emphasize the best features of every home."

—Kathleen Pettit, author, producer, community organizer

"Diane Keyes has been an important part of my marketing plan for the last fifteen years. She has prepared hundreds of my listings, helping them to sell quickly and more profitably. Other realtors often compliment me on how well my listings show. The reason is clear—Diane Keyes. Following the advice in this book is the best investment you'll ever make in your home."

—Mary Sommerfeld, Master's Circle Realtor®

"A must-read for all realtors who call themselves professionals, this book can help give you that competitive edge."

—Peggy Sparr, Realtor®

"Pay close attention to the advice that Diane Keyes gives in *This Sold House*. Our own house sold for full price in three days after following Diane's suggestions! You will find no one better qualified and with more experience to help you prepare your home for sale. Homeowners, real estate professionals, and investors alike will benefit from the insight and common sense in *This Sold House*."

—Andi Saylor, CRP and author of *ON THE MOVE: The Complete Guide to Relocating* www.relocatinghelp.com

"If you are one of the millions of people who will sell their home this year, this book is an absolute must-have! I always thought that getting my house ready for sale meant spending lots of money—not true! As Diane Keyes points out, it's not about having the right stuff that's so important—it's having your stuff in the right place! Diane takes you step-by-step through the whole process of getting MORE money for your home—and isn't that what selling your home is all about?"

—Colleen Szot, author, TV scriptwriter

"*This Sold House* clearly describes our own experience. After having been on the market for eight months without selling, we took Diane's advice and our home sold in less than one week. The first person who saw the house bought it! Diane's uncanny ability to recommend simple changes to enable a successful sale made an immediate and striking difference. We highly recommend Diane as well as her book."

—Suzan McGinnis, attorney, collections librarian

"The book is excellent. Really, I was captivated, I couldn't put it down. I read every word as soon as I received it! *This Sold House* is IT!"

—Linda Mershon, corporate manager

"Nice work, Diane! I've been a commercial interior designer for ten years, but staging a house for sale is a different ballgame."

—Beth Crumbaker CID (Commercial Interior Designer) and project manager

"We did everything on Diane's list except for one thing and we sold our home the day it went on the market, even though there were two homes on our street that had been for sale for six months. The buyer's agent actually asked if he could bring his girlfriend over to see the best-staged home he'd seen in his twenty years of real estate!"

—Caroline Severson, mortgage associate

"I highly recommend Diane's book. I always thought that staging was just about making the property look pretty, nicely decorated, or simply neat and tidy. As Diane points out, it also means removing obstacles, increasing the sense of space and flow, neutralizing decorating extremes, anticipating potential buyer objections, and most importantly getting inside the head of the buyer. She brings a whole new dimension to staging with her understanding of the psychology of a home sale. You'll attract more buyers with *This Sold House*."

—Jeff Jackson, Mortgage Lender, Durango, Colorado

"Diane has a wonderfully perceptive way of not only seeing the problems and potential, but also tapping into the spirit of a space and its occupants. Filled with great suggestions and attention-grabbing stories that make everything more real because we can all relate to them, I'll remember *This Sold House* when it's time for us to leave the home we love so much."

—Ken Ekstein, LISW; social worker, artist, environmentalist

"With logical, easy-to-understand instructions, *This Sold House* is the best-written book I have seen on staging. Sellers that implement her suggestions will sell their homes more quickly and for more money than those who don't. If you are preparing to sell your home, this book is a must-read."

—Dan Burt, Realtor®

"We followed her advice and the results were dramatic. The things we changed were not expensive, but still allowed us to transform the house into an inviting space in just three weeks while we both worked full-time. The house sold the first weekend, at list price, with multiple offers."

—Suzanne Egan and Cort Martin, homeowners

"*This Sold House* clearly shows you how to help any potential buyer see your home's real space and its potential, not its problems. It's a quick read, full of workable common sense and clear, concise information designed to help sellers understand what an important part they play in the sale of their home. The solutions Diane offers are easy, inexpensive, and empower you to become your home's best advocate. She speaks with a new voice, and it's a voice that needs to be heard in today's challenging market."

—Cheryl Meyer, photographer

"Diane helped us quickly sell two houses over the past year. There's both an art and a science to staging your house for a quick, full-value sale. Trust an expert with a proven track record and follow her advice!"

—Aaron Latto, second vice president, Travelers Insurance

"*This Sold House* would be extremely beneficial for sellers to have before listing their homes, and it's a great gift to give sellers when doing a market analysis for them."

—Sheryl Vogesser, Realtor®

"Geared toward getting the most revenue from a sale using everyday common sense ideas, this book should be required reading for all agents."

—Bill Ivory, Realtor®

"This book is truly a JOY. Every seller needs this step-by-step guide to making their home irresistible to potential buyers; its pages are filled with priceless and easy-to-take advice for the quickest sale at the highest profit. *This Sold House* a quick and enjoyable read; some of her anecdotes are so funny that I laughed out loud. Sellers will be left feeling optimistic and more empowered with each turn of the page —you won't want to make a move without her."

—Jane Duden, educational consultant, author and educator

This
SOLD
House

*Staging Your Home to Sell
in Today's Market*

Diane Keyes

THIRD CHILD
PRESS

This Sold House
Staging Your Home to Sell in Today's Market
by Diane Keyes

Published by:

 Third Child Press
P.O. Box 32092
Minneapolis, MN 55432 U.S.A.

Sales@ThisSoldHouse.biz
http://www.thissoldhouse.biz

Unattributed quotations are by Diane Keyes

Cover design and interior layout by Purpose Design

ISBN, print ed. 978-0-9767999-0-0
ISBN, PDF ed. 978-0-9767999-1-7

1st ed.

Library of Congress Cataloging-in-Publication Data
Keyes, Diane.
This sold house: staging your home to sell in today's market / Diane Keyes
p.cm.
LCCN 2008900947
ISBN-13: 978-0-9767999-0-0
ISBN-10: 0-9767999-0-1
ISBN-13: 978-0-9767999-1-7
ISBN-10: 0-9767999-1-X

1. Home staging. 2. House selling–United States.
I. Title.

HD1375.K49 2008   333.33'83
                    QBI08-600112

This book is designed to provide information on home staging and preparing a home for sale. It is sold with the understanding that the publisher and author are not engaged in rendering legal, real estate brokerage or other professional services. If legal or other expert assistance is required, the services of a competent professional should be sought.

The purpose of this book is to educate and entertain. The author and Third Child Press shall have neither liability nor responsibility to any person or entity with respect to any loss or damage caused, or alleged to have been caused, directly or indirectly, by the information contained in this book.

If you do not wish to be bound by the above, you may return this book to the publisher for a full refund.

This book is available at quantity discounts for bulk purchases. For information please email sales@ thissoldhouse.biz

Contents

Foreword

Our homes are intensely personal and as such we take great care in decorating them to reflect who we are. However, our personal decorating style can actually get in the way when it's time to sell because it can deter buyers who don't share our individual taste. In *This Sold House*, Diane Keyes shows us how easy it is to identify and correct those problems to increase the number of interested buyers— so critical in today's saturated housing market.

Diane points out that it's not only what we see, but what we don't see in our homes that can make buyers turn and run, and she explains how to return the focus to the house, not the decorating, to make our homes more marketable to the masses.

But *This Sold House* is more than just a how-to approach to staging homes. Diane addresses the emotional issues tied to letting go of our homes. She looks at the how and why of things we may be doing to unintentionally sabotage the sale.

Diane shares her tips for maximizing space and minimizing flaws. She gives specific examples for creating an enticing environment, from what to put in a window box to what music to play—as well as fabulous room-by-room tips that help show the space in its best light.

Much like a makeup artist or a wardrobe stylist does for an actor or actress, Diane helps homeowners accentuate the positive features of their homes while diminishing the negatives.

She has funneled her years of experience into a common sense approach that anyone can understand and apply to create a stage that will allow potential buyers to envision your house as their new home.

This Sold House is a must-have for anyone considering a move in this challenging market.

—*Teresa Meyer, producer, Edelman Productions, HGTV*

Acknowledgements

I have many people to thank because I'm blessed to be surrounded by the best friends and family imaginable. My thanks to:

Cheryl Meyer, my soul sister, who continued to tell me I was ready until I was.

Jolene Gauss, for always challenging me to move forward.

Jane Mitchell, for her example and her faith in me.

Steve Greenwell and Ken Eckstein, and Lynne and Pat Schriver-Sheedy, for all their love and support.

Dottie Stack, my dear friend and business partner.

Mary Sommerfeld, who has not only used my services for twenty years, but has been my one-woman marketing team.

Andi Saylor, whose kind invitation opened so many doors for me.

Connie Anderson, for being a great editor, mentor, and friend.

Colleen Szot, for her optimism, assistance and friendship.

Mary Jo Sherwood, for her generous heart and unerring expertise.

The other Women of Words, whose welcome, help, and inspiration brought me the rest of the way.

Harry and Sharon Stockhausen, for their advice and guidance.

Heidi Koopman at Purpose Design, for her commitment to excellence, her kindness and her perfect timing.

My indescribably wonderful family, for all the years of support and encouragement.

My mom who always told me it would happen.

My daughter, Kelsey, who spent countless hours helping me write and rewrite and photograph this book, and whose creative spirit is a delight to me.

My son, Troy, who told me I was talented in such a heartfelt way he made me believe it and whose own talent blows me away.

And my husband Tom, like everything good in our lives, we've listened, spoken, and believed it into being.

Introduction

It all began with a frantic phone call from my mother. "Do something, Diane," Mom said. "You've got to stop Gary and Katie from buying that house. It will be the worst mistake of their lives."

My mother's few words, uttered about my brother's new purchase, created a light-bulb moment for me and provided the inspiration for a home-staging career I've enjoyed since the mid '80s.

My brother and his wife were buying a great house. It was a 100-year-old Scandinavian rectory, with kitchen cupboards and bookcases made by the best cabinetmakers in town. This one-of-a-kind property had stained glass tulips in the front door, a view of the lake, two fireplaces, built-in corner cupboards, and charming architectural details in every room.

I fell in love with this gracious old home and gave Gary and Katie a thumbs-up on their choice.

"Mom doesn't think that we should buy the house. She thinks it's a nightmare," he said, "but we don't see the problem."

The problem was Mom couldn't see any of the home's fabulous features and potential. She saw an entirely different house.

Mom saw the ugly, old, royal blue drapes on every window that blocked the view of the lake and made the house dark and depressing.

She saw the awful wallpaper in the bedroom, the basement full of smelly, dirty, hip-deep laundry, and the piles of junk that covered the beautiful maple flooring and completely hid the fireplace. In her eyes, it was a disaster.

Despite Mom's protests, Gary and Katie bought the house anyway. On moving day we sent every royal blue drape to the dumpster and threw open all the French windows. It only took minutes for our family moving crew to remove the ugly wallpaper in the master bedroom, so old it literally fell off the walls. And happily for us, the previous owners took the dirty laundry and the smell with them.

With the walls and windows bare, the bedrooms felt bigger and sunlight flooded the space. The additional light opened up every room, revealing the home's charm and many possibilities.

Mom was amazed when she came over to bring supper the day we moved my brother and his family into their new home. And I was amazed when I realized how few changes were needed to entirely alter the visual impact of a property.

It wasn't long before I began helping sellers make changes that increase the visual impact of their homes so they sell faster and command a higher price.

And now in *This Sold House*, I'm sharing the secrets with you. Developed over my twenty years experience staging homes, these techniques have helped my clients sell their homes—and will help you too, no matter what is happening in the real estate market.

Using the elements of space, light, and color, along with a little psychology, you'll be able to make your home as inviting and appealing as possible. And created with the average homeowner in mind, my simple approach doesn't require any design expertise.

My house-staging ideas help you arrange your furnishings to reveal your home's best features and eliminate the distractions and visual clutter that keep buyers from *seeing* the space—in person or on the internet. My **Quick Tips** throughout the book give you shortcuts to getting great results. And my real-life stories are intended to make you laugh and help you understand the concepts necessary to successfully prepare your home for the market. Combine the **Keys to a Quick Sale** with my **Three Simple Questions** and **Seven Staging Secrets** and you have all the ingredients necessary to produce your own *best-seller*.

You see, most people are like my mom. They see only what's right in front of them. They want to visualize how they'll fit into a home, but often they can't get past the distractions. Remove the distractions and buyers can more easily see the space and imagine themselves living in it. And once you engage their imagination, potential buyers are more likely to make your space—their space.

With my proven methods and your motivation, we've got a winning team and you've got a house to sell. So, let's get moving!

ONE

Don't Make a Move Without Me

Want to sell your home quickly and for the best price in today's buyers' market? Make it more attractive to buyers.

Even though the market may change, the houses that sell the fastest and for the highest price have a lot in common. They are cleaner, better organized, and less cluttered than the other homes for sale in their price range and location. In short, they're more attractive to buyers. It's not having the *right* stuff that's so important; it's having the *right amount* of stuff in the *right place*, sending the *right* visual cues.

Not long ago, I consulted on a two-story home in a beautiful older neighborhood, the house had great features but they were buried under several years of neglect. The day after my visit, the Realtor® phoned to say he was sorry he hadn't called me before he'd set the listing price and put the house on the market. After my two-hour consultation with the homeowner, the Realtor® believed the listing price should have been set at $210,000 instead of the $175,000 price they'd chosen. That's an additional $35,000 in the listing price and a possible 20 percent increase in the profit! All without spending one nickel on the property.

What made the house $35,000 more valuable than it was two hours earlier? It became more valuable because we eliminated the distractions and traffic flow problems that kept the charm of the house from showing through. The house was worth more on the real estate market because it became more *visually attractive* to buyers. I helped the homeowner *reveal the true value of the home.*

When you make a property more attractive to buyers, you increase its salability. When you increase the salability, you increase the number of potential buyers. When you increase the number of potential buyers, you *decrease* the length of time the house stays on the market and you *increase* the price buyers are willing to pay.

Today's marketplace is a visual one where perception is reality and appearance is everything. These days, the real estate battle cry not only shouts *location, location, location*—it screams *appearance, appearance, appearance.* Staging homes to help them sell is no longer optional—it's a necessity.

Along with making their homes more attractive in person, today's home sellers must first attract buyers on the Internet. Having grown up with computers, most of today's buyers are visual junkies, so how a home looks on the Internet is crucial to its saleability. Sellers can no longer rely on their home's in-person appeal or the neighborhood's charm to get buyers in the door. Today, 86 percent of buyers see a home on a computer screen and say yes or no with the click of a keypad before ever scheduling a showing.

Unfortunately for many homeowners, how a house looks in person is not necessarily the same as how it appears on the Internet. If not well-staged, even the loveliest homes can look unattractive in a small, grainy Internet picture. And if you try to list your home without pictures on-line, potential buyers assume you have something to hide and pass you by. With several times as many houses on the market as there are buyers in most locations, no one worries about running out of available properties.

Homeowners aren't just selling homes—they are in a marketing competition and they need professional help. With so much at stake, many people feel completely overwhelmed by all the questions that arise when selling their home.

- When should the house go on the market?
- What should the listing price be?
- How much work should be done before selling the home?
- What changes are needed outside to create curb appeal?
- Should the floors be re-carpeted or is it enough to provide a carpeting allowance?
- And on, and on, and on.

It's no wonder moving is considered one of life's twenty most stressful events. And making it even *more trying*, one of the top five stressors—death, divorce, illness, job loss or a financial setback—is often the reason for a change of residence. Add today's mortgage crisis to the mix and you have real stress!

Real estate professionals and clients agree that my process reduces listing time and increases the market value of a home without the costly investment required by other staging services. My own analysis shows that when the techniques I share in the book are used, the listing time is reduced by more than 50 percent, and there is an average 1.5–2 percent increase in the sale price of the home as a result of the shorter listing time.

Using the earlier example where the listing price of the house jumped from $175,000 to $210,000 after my visit, the numbers work out like this. If the house sells for $175,000, the profit would average out to be $2,625 with a 1.5 percent increase in the sale price or $3,500 with a 2 percent increase. However, if you were to have made the changes *before* the listing price was set, you would realize between $3,150 and $4,200 for the increase in the sale price and an additional $35,000 for the increase in the listing price, making a total increase of $38,150 to $39,200! A nice profit for a few dollars and a little effort!

While every area is different and my numbers specifically reflect the greater Minneapolis/St. Paul area, you will see your investment return many times over when you *reveal* the true value of your home, *reduce* your listing time, and *raise* your profits by applying the secrets in *This Sold House*!

TWO

Yes, You Can

Now, let's get started. Whether you're aware of it or not, you are already an expert because no one knows your home better than you.

If you are questioning something about your home that might need changing—*it most likely does*. Chances are if something is bothering you, it's likely to bother a potential buyer as well. It could be crumbling front steps or a sofa blocking the view to the garden. It could be the bookcase that keeps your pass-through from being a pass-through, peeling paint, missing floorboards, or the bedroom your son painted black during his Goth period. It could be, and probably is, exactly what you're thinking about at this very moment.

Whether it's the front steps, the view-blocking sofa, or the black bedroom, following your first response will put you on the right track towards making improvements that will help your home sell quickly.

The more rooms you stage, the greater the impact on potential buyers, but remember it's not expected or even necessary to use every suggestion I mention. It is the cumulative effect of many changes that's important. No *one* idea is sacred unless there's something that can't be overlooked—like your son's black bedroom. Then my advice is to get out the paint and roller.

The Ten Essentials Steps

Now let's map out a plan. Here are the **Ten Essentials Steps** you need to begin organizing your home for the real estate market.

One—*Make a list.*

Make a list of what you think needs to be done starting with the front yard and working your way through the house in the direction you think it will be shown.

If possible, bring buyers into your home through your front door. Front doors and entries are usually larger and provide a more inviting environment for first-time visitors. Ask your agent to put the lockbox on the door you would like your potential buyers to use to enter your home.

Two—*Focus on completing the easiest, quickest items on the list.*

Spend a day or two on the tasks that are the most quickly and easily done. Working on small manageable projects will give you a feeling of control and accomplishment that will carry you through the more difficult, time-consuming tasks. It also allows you to make the most changes in the least amount of time.

Three—*Prioritize your list by determining which of the remaining items could cause you to lose a sale.*

These items are the most obvious problems, the things that, although they are not necessarily expensive to fix, might keep someone from buying your home or being seriously interested because they send a negative message.

An example from my own home was a broken piece of trim on the bottom of the window visitors walked past when coming to our front door. Even though it made a terrible first impression and it only cost a few dollars to replace, we didn't take the time to fix it until we decided to sell our home.

Four—*Tackle the items at the top of your list, concentrating on the areas buyers will see first on their visit to your home.*

Correcting the most noticeable things first will keep buyers from seeing a problem at the beginning of their visit. If they see a concern right away, it's more likely to hinder the sale.

Five—*Do one task at a time.*

No matter what you've heard about multitasking, most people who multitask aren't more productive. They just feel busier and more stressed so they think they must be getting more done.

Six—*Handle things only once.*

When you pick something up, put it down where it belongs. If you are struggling with a decision about what to do with something, put it in a box marked "undecided." Then move it out of sight, so it's off your radar.

Seven—*Make changes that are easy to live with while you're still in your home.*

Don't take all the leaves out of the dining room table and move all the chairs to the basement if you're having your family over for dinner this weekend. Remember: Usually it's the combined effect of all the changes you make that is important, rather than one killer idea.

Eight—*Cross items off your list as you do them.*

Seeing progress is very satisfying and will help motivate you to do the next thing on the list.

Nine—*Set realistic expectations and stick to your list.*

If you think of other things you'd like to do, put them on a separate list and consider them later, after you've finished with your essential list.

Ten—*Keep things simple.*

Then relax, have confidence in your choices, and imagine your buyer walking through the door at any moment.

THREE

What Buyers and Sellers Are Really Thinking

Before you begin to implement your list, it's important to understand a bit about the mindset of today's buyers and sellers. Most people buy homes based on how they feel about a home, not how it's decorated. Their feelings come from a place inside them that holds all their memories and defines what *home* means to them. Over the years, I've talked to hundreds of people who told me they just *knew* when they pulled up to the house or walked in the front door that a certain house was meant for them.

Buying a home is an emotional response. *It's about psychology, not decorating.* How else can you explain that it can take months to pick out a sofa, but only a couple short visits to buy a house? Most folks spend more time choosing their furniture than the living room they're going to put it in.

A buyer purchases a house because it *feels* right, not because they have examined every square inch and found it perfect. However, what is going on in the sellers' psyche is quite different. Sellers evaluate their homes through the rose-colored glasses of nostalgia.

The seller's inner dialogue goes like this:

"I know no one else in the neighborhood has gotten as much as we are asking for our home, but it really is the best house in town. All it needs is a little work and some paint.

"Just look at those marks on the inside of the kitchen archway where we measured the kids' height every year; it seems like only yesterday. I probably should paint, but the new owners most likely wouldn't like my paint colors anyway.

"After all, that's part of the fun of buying a new house— coming in and making it your own. I'll accept a little lower price so they can fix things up for themselves and choose their own paint colors.

"I know that some of the branches of that big old tree in the backyard are resting on the roof and the tree should probably be cut down, but I remember the kids playing on their tire swing and jumping into leaf piles in the fall.

"This has been a wonderful home, I'm sure people will fall in love with it, just the way we did!"

The seller's view is based on emotion, sweet memories, and rationalization. They believe they are making a rational judgment about their home when they are really expressing their feelings. Sellers are biased and believe their home is worth as much to buyers as it is worth to them.

The seller is selling a home.

The buyer is buying a property.

It is how *the buyer feels* about the house that counts.

The potential buyer's inner dialogue sounds more like this:

"This house is cute, but it looks like it's been neglected. The color is fine, but the Internet photos didn't show that the paint is peeling. And all those marks on the side of the kitchen archway, I can't believe they didn't bother to paint over them.

"I just don't feel comfortable buying a house that looks as if it hasn't been maintained. I'll keep looking until I find one that feels right. I'll know it when I find the right house for me. And that big old tree in the backyard—some of the branches rest right on the roof! I wouldn't be surprised if the roof needs replacing. I bet, in the fall, all they do is rake leaves.

"If they don't care enough to fix the things people can see, I wonder what else is wrong. Besides, they're asking more for this property than other homes in this neighborhood. There are lots more houses for sale, I may as well look at the others instead."

Buyers look for visual cues. Whether a seller admits it or not, condition, care, and cleanliness (or the lack thereof) are the subtle visual cues that register with buyers. **Prospective buyers make assumptions about your house based on *what they see* and *how they feel* about what they see.**

It's unlikely you'll have the opportunity to explain why you haven't taken down that old tree or why you haven't painted. Instead, buyers assume the house has not been maintained—and move on to another property.

The Problem With Perfection

In the same way that obvious problems are trouble, so is perfection. Some of the most difficult houses to sell look like a page out of *Better*

Homes and Gardens. While having your home in perfect condition is important, having your home perfectly decorated is not.

Why are these well-decorated homes often so hard to sell? There are several reasons:

- With a perfectly decorated home, it's easy for buyers to wonder whether the charm is in the home's decorating or the house itself. They may worry that when the sellers remove their lovely furnishings, the house could lose the appeal it had before.

- Potential buyers can also be distracted by *things* instead of focusing on the space itself. It's a lot like visiting a museum. People usually remember the treasures inside, not the rooms that held them. If your rooms are beautifully filled with things, it's more difficult for the buyer to focus on the space. *If buyers don't see the space, they won't buy the space.*

- In addition, when a home is perfectly decorated, the owner's personal style will limit the home's appeal to only those buyers who like or can relate to that particular style rather than keeping it open to a variety of potential buyers. Your home may be impeccably furnished with very modern furniture and accessories, such as geometric patterns, leather, and chrome. Or it may be exquisitely done with a bold new British Colonial design, and you may love the sophistication of the décor. But if the potential buyers don't share your taste they'll keep looking.

- Your style of decorating may also prevent potential buyers from being able to picture themselves living in your house. It's difficult for people to imagine their own belongings in a space that's already perfect.

Happily dreaming of one's own things in new surroundings provides a great deal of motivation for the buyer. If a buyer is thinking, "My table will fit perfectly here, and this corner is just right for the

Christmas tree, and if I put my desk there I'll overlook the pond when I work," you're likely to sell your home.

On the other hand if the buyer is thinking, "This place is gorgeous, do you suppose that painting is an original? This room wouldn't look near as nice with my crummy old desk and saggy sofa," you're much less likely to see a sale.

All these factors affect the salability of your home. If you are looking for a fast and profitable sale, it is in your best interest to appeal to the *largest* number of potential buyers, not just those who like and are comfortable with your favorite design style.

Warning: Too Much Information
May Cause System Failure

I'm often invited to make presentations at realtors' sales meetings. One such gathering for real estate professionals who specialize in expensive properties was held at a new $1,500,000 listing. It was an older home, built by a banker baron, set on several wooded acres and overlooking a beautiful lake.

I'd been surprised at what I considered to be a reasonable price for the quality of the property and the location—until I arrived. To say the decorating was over the top doesn't begin to do it justice. It was astonishing.

To give you just a few of the highlights: An antique Model T sat in the living room on a lighted glass floor, and a full-size robotic French chef stood in the corner of the kitchen. The garage had hand-painted silk wallpaper, beautiful Persian rugs, wingback chairs, and a silk sofa. The décor was nicely lit by a dozen crystal sconces on the garage walls.

Each room was more elaborate than the last, and I'm sure the furnishings were actually more valuable than the house itself. After we had all toured the house I began my talk.

"I'd like to start by asking who can tell me how many bedrooms this home has?" The room fell silent. Then laughter rippled through the room as thirty-five real estate agents (with a combined total of at least five hundred years of real estate experience) realized, much to their embarrassment, that none of them could tell me how many bedrooms were in the house.

The banker baron home wasn't huge by estate standards. There were only three bedrooms—all grouped nicely together in the bedroom wing. However, people can only absorb so much, and if too much information is coming in, there are no brain circuits left for recording, imagining—or anything else for that matter.

Quick Tip

Ask your real estate agent what potential buyers are saying when they leave your home. If they are talking about furnishings instead of features, they are probably not thinking about buying your home. You may need to consider bringing your personal style down a notch so it will appeal to a wider market.

Sometimes sellers are reluctant to make changes, even when they know that without them, it may be more difficult to sell their home. It's not uncommon for homeowners to feel ambivalent about putting their home on the market although they're committed to doing so. It's never easy to say good-bye.

When homeowners have invested time and money creating a home, or they are not ready to move on from the life they've lived there, they can be reluctant to leave even though they know they must. It can be hard to imagine living life in entirely different surroundings.

In addition, many people making a move are not doing it by choice. Two-thirds of the time a major stressor such as death, divorce, job loss or transfer, illness, or financial setback precipitates the decision to move. It's not easy to leave the home you shared with your now-deceased spouse, or to move on after the love of your life has found another partner. And it's difficult to admit you no longer can physically care for your home or afford to remain there. Even if you move for joyous reasons, such as the birth of a longed-for child, you are still leaving a part of your life behind.

The Ties That Bind

I recently did a consultation for clients in such a situation. Jim and Erica were eagerly awaiting the birth of twins—their third and fourth children. In addition, Erica had just received a six-figure advance on her second book. They were elated. Currently strapped for space in a small two-bedroom ranch house, they were now able to make their dreams come true. They'd put a contingent offer on a beautiful new home in a nice neighborhood closer to Jim's office.

They should have been ecstatic, but I sensed ambivalence. The reason knocked on the door while I was there. Erica's parents and chief babysitters lived right down the block, and they all loved their intergenerational living situation. It was only after an unsuccessful attempt to get a remodeling variance that Erica and Jim decided to sell their home. For three months, it sat on the market with hardly a showing. Then a large home, four doors away from their folks, went up for sale. Jim and Erica snapped it up. Within a week their old home sold.

Over the years, I've noticed it's quite common for a perfectly lovely house to linger on the market, while a less-attractive, similarly priced, or even *more* expensive home on the same block sells right away.

When homeowners say they're anxious to move, but are still emotionally tied to the home, their strong feelings can unintentionally send the unspoken message to buyers that the house is not really available to them. The homeowners' ambivalent feelings, their *owner energy*, can actually keep the house from selling.

Real estate agents tell me they can often tell just walking up to the front door if the current owners are not ready to let go of the house. And if owners aren't ready to leave their home, then the best real estate agent or home stager in the world won't be able to sell it.

More Ties That Bind

I try not to take it personally, but sometimes real estate agents don't contact me until they're at the end of their rope. One desperate call was from a Realtor® with a listing he just could not sell. It was a nice, affordable home in a good neighborhood, it was fairly priced, and he didn't understand why it hadn't sold.

He was also disturbed by the owner's lack of cooperation. It seems she would find reasons to stay home whenever the agent brought buyers through the house. The owner was also cooking every time the agent showed the property—and she wasn't filling the house with buyer-enticing smells. She was cooking cabbage and even frying fish!

After listening to the Realtor® vent for a while, I asked the circumstances of the owner's move. The owner was a widowed young mom, with serious financial problems that made it necessary for her to sell.

Having facilitated grief groups, I suspected she was not ready to leave her home. I gave the Realtor® a short course on listening and bereavement and suggested he spend some time just listening to her. Within a couple weeks he called to say the house was sold. The only thing this young woman needed was to feel heard in expressing her grief.

I've visited with many owners who, like this young widow, signed the papers but were not ready to sell their homes. I can often tell when sellers aren't ready to leave because most of the time they are unwilling to make even small changes in their environments.

On one occasion, I visited with a woman who was so conflicted about her decision that she argued with every suggestion I made. After she vetoed virtually all of my recommendations, we talked about her reluctance. I explained that her resistance to change indicated to me she might not be ready to sell her home.

She admitted that she'd recently been divorced and resented having to move from a home she loved because it was too large to care for by herself. With her ambivalent feelings about moving, I thought it was unlikely the house would sell. I suggested she take some time to think about whether she really was ready to move and then we could get together again.

The real estate agent was not surprised when I told her about my visit with the homeowner. The listing had been signed and cancelled three times. Aware that her efforts to sell the house would be in vain if the buyer was not ready to move, the agent was relieved that her client's resistance was finally being discussed openly.

Feelings, such as doubt, fear, or ambivalence are normal. Anytime you move to a new place, you are leaving a piece of your life behind. Whether you've experienced a great loss or you're moving to celebrate a wonderful event, the transition can still be difficult.

If you think you may not be ready to let go of your home and move on to a new phase of your life, I encourage you to share your concerns with someone. Often, just talking with a priest, minister, trusted friend, or family member can be all you need to be able to process your feelings and reach closure. It's better to resolve your issues than put the house on the market before you are ready to say yes to the new life in store for you.

To help make the emotional transition, give yourself and your home a farewell party. Surround yourself with loved ones and share your memories of good times with family and friends, asking for blessings on the new owners. These rites of passage make it easier to move and will reassure you there are wonderful memories yet to come.

The book of life has many chapters, each filled with opportunities for love, joy, fun, and adventure. It would be a shame to come to the end of your life with the book unfinished. Savor the chapter you're reading—then turn the page.

FOUR

Keys to a Quick Sale

As you read through this chapter you will find my **Keys to a Quick Sale**—the secrets I've discovered that will unlock your door to a quick, profitable sale. After years in the business, I have noticed that no matter what is happening in the market, these key concepts are consistently true. And, they're more important than ever in the competitive market we're facing today.

The keys are illustrated with stories to make it easier for you to remember, understand, and apply these principles to your home. Although the stories are true, the names have been changed for obvious reasons.

1

Quick Sale Key

When preparing your home for sale,
make sure your home is in peak selling condition
before it goes on the market.

Color Me Stunned

Over the years I've found it fascinating that people choose to ignore their best instincts when putting their homes on the market.

One of my most memorable consultations was on a house that had already been for sale a long time when I was called. Violet and Red Hughes, the friendly owners, greeted me warmly at the door, before I even had a chance to knock.

"We're so anxious to sell," Violet said, "we have a home waiting for us in Hill City, and we can't afford to make payments on both places." Their real estate agent stood near his clients with a stricken look on his face.

"I'm so glad you're here, Diane. Really glad," he pumped my hand eagerly, unwilling to let go now that I'd arrived. I'm sure he knew what the problem was, but seemed embarrassed to discuss something so obvious—afraid that it would insult or offend his sellers.

Even though I could see they were desperate to sell, they were blind to the very obvious reason for the lack of buyers, but it was apparent to me. When I came into the Hughes' home, their decorating style was so bold it hurt to look.

"Are you okay, Diane?" Violet asked.

"I'm fine," I answered weakly. I guess I looked as dizzy as I felt.

It was like looking through a kaleidoscope. Royal blue and red translucent paint adorned the glass front door that led into the living room, which was carpeted with a bright blue and red swirl-patterned shag rug. Two living room walls were painted baby blue and the other two sported gold and cream fleur-de-lis flocked wallpaper.

But the decorating nightmare didn't end there. The kitchen basked in the glow of sunburst yellow walls; yellow, orange, and lime-green flowered wallpaper; green and yellow plaid linoleum; and road-construction orange countertops. But the pièce de résistance was the purple patterned carpet in the hallway between the kitchen and living room. All of these colors, yes, you read it right, all of them, with the exception of the orange countertops, were visible as soon as you opened the front door.

It looked like Walt Disney had a nuclear meltdown right there in the living room. Unfortunately, the fallout from the explosion spread all through the entire house.

I was stunned, as I'm sure all the prospective buyers had been. And although I didn't run screaming from the house as buyers surely must have, I did excuse myself to go to the bathroom, where I threw cold water on my face and planned my escape.

When I recovered enough to emerge, I looked past the cacophony of colors and discovered lifesaving hardwood floors under all the carpet. Fortunately, I convinced the owners that oak flooring makes a great selling feature, especially when accompanied by cream-colored walls.

"We wondered if we should paint," Violet said. "But we thought the new owners might want to choose their own colors." This is seller-speak for "it's too darned much work."

"Your current palette keeps prospective buyers from being able to see your space," I said tactfully.

Red and Violet were very skeptical, but the house had been on the market so long they were willing to try anything. They made the necessary changes, and the house sold immediately. They realized that, although they loved their kaleidoscope home and had taken good care of it, the home did reflect their own uniquely colorful view of life.

Your *first* potential buyers provide the *easiest, fastest, and most profitable* sales opportunities. Most often, they are the folks who are interested in buying a house in your neighborhood and keep track of homes in the area that are currently on the market. Or they may be people who drive by *your* home regularly because something about it appeals to them.

These potential buyers are already sold on the location and the outward appearance of the house. Now they want to like what's inside as well. *Don't let them down!* Make sure they see your home at its best.

The biggest mistake people make is to put the house on the market "as is" to see what happens. Often nothing happens, except those first *most likely* buyers leave disappointed, and the house remains on the market so long that the only way to increase interest in the house is by lowering the asking price.

As Violet and Red learned, you pay a price for putting your home on the market "as is," because *the faster the sale, the higher the price.*

2

Quick Sale Key

Make the improvements and changes
before you set your listing price.

Do What I Say, Not What I Did

*I am ashamed to say that I didn't take that advice when my own home was for sale. My old carpet was very expensive because I'd purchased it wholesale. I reasoned that people would prefer old expensive carpeting rather than have new, less expensive flooring. I violated my own cardinal rule—**perception is reality**. The reality is that the old carpeting looked dark, dreary and dated, while new carpeting would look light, fresh, and clean.*

Time and again homeowners say to me, "I know the carpeting is old and worn but I don't want to go to the trouble of replacing it. I'll be happy to give the new owners a carpeting allowance."

This approach would work well if it brought in buyers. However, this is what happens every time improvements aren't made before trying to sell the house: The sellers put the house on the market with the old carpet and adjust the listing price down because the carpet needs replacing. Potential buyers come and go. Finally the sellers surrender and purchase new carpeting. Unfortunately, by this time they have probably lowered the list price trying to create more interest and attract buyers. Instead of taking a single hit for the price of new carpet, they take three hits: the lower initial price, the listing price reduction because of the length of time on the market, and the price of the carpet they ended up buying anyway.

I estimate we may have lost as much as $20,000 by not buying new carpet before the house went on the market. The cost of the carpet was only $2,400, but we lowered the listing price before we gave in and bought new carpet.

Our home sold to the third couple that walked in the door after we replaced the carpet.

Making your improvements and changes before setting the listing price will result in the highest possible listing price and a higher sale price as well. It also guarantees your home will be ready to capture those first purchase-ready buyers. Remember:

- Penny wise, pound foolish.

- A stitch in time saves nine.

- An ounce of prevention is worth a pound of cure.

- Perception is reality.

3
Quick Sale Key

Homes sell more easily
if they fit well into the neighborhood.

One of These Things Is Not Like the Other

"The house is in immaculate condition and in a great neighborhood," the agent said when she called to ask if I would consult on her newest listing. "It's small, but I think that's really an advantage because the neighborhood is so desirable it's the only way for a young family to buy into the area. I can't put my finger on it, but I have a feeling it may be difficult to sell. Could you come pinpoint the problem for me?"

When I got there I didn't even need to get out of the car to see what was wrong. The house, though cute as a button, did not fit the neighborhood. The house on one side of it was a traditional Georgian style two-story home, symmetrical and tasteful, with white siding and gray trim. The home on the other side was a story and a half bungalow, painted gray with white trim.

The house in question was a small '50's bungalow. The house was painted sage green with yellow trim. It had blue shutters and a pink door. It was very cute, too cute. It looked like a Barbie dream house and the fantasy extended to the front garden, awash with whirligigs and plastic critters, gnomes, and toadstools.

Making matters worse, instead of a small mailbox mounted on the front of the house like everyone within miles, the homeowner had placed a rural mailbox on a post by the front door and decorated it with bee, bird, and butterfly decals.

We made some changes indoors, but it was clear that the exterior décor was the real problem. When we got to the front yard, I could tell the owner expected me to rave about her wonderland.

Taking a deep breath I said, "I wouldn't be honest if I didn't give you all my ideas."

Then, as diplomatically as possible, I explained that the style of her home did not fit well into the neighborhood setting and pointed out the absence of pointy-toed gnomes, plastic mushrooms, and pastels in the neighboring yards. I could see she was unhappy, but in all fairness to her, she did listen and agreed to remove a few of the plastic mushrooms, gnomes, and some of the other cutesy things in the garden. However, she said no way to my painting suggestions.

She said a cordial good-bye, but I wasn't surprised when she didn't wave.

I saw the agent recently and she told me the house stayed on the market for a couple months before the owner painted the trim and the front door, replaced the mailbox, and de-plasticized the front yard. Then it sold right away.

When selling your house, whether you're talking about the color, the landscaping, or the style, the best choice for your home is the look that fits in with the rest of the neighborhood. Part of the home sale package is your neighborhood, so your home will be more attractive to prospective buyers if it looks like it belongs in its setting.

A geodesic dome in a neighborhood of traditional homes, a large two-story colonial in a ranch development, a log home in the city, are all examples of homes out of their element.

Unfortunately for their owners, if the architectural style of the house is unlike the rest of the neighborhood, I am often unable to do much to change its outward appearance. Owners just have to trust that a buyer with a taste for originality will find them.

If that's the case, however, there's even more reason to stage the home so that there will be as few objections to the rest of the house as possible. All many homes need is a pinch here and a tuck there to make them fit perfectly into their environment.

4
Quick Sale Key
The sale is in the details.

Splatter Where?

By the time the Realtor® called me to visit her listing in one of the more upscale suburbs of our area, it had already been on the market for a couple of months.

When I asked Jane what she thought the problem was, she replied, "I'm not really sure, Diane. The market is really hot right now and the house is lovely. I thought it would be snapped up right away. Would you mind taking a look?"

Jane was right; the house was lovely—well-decorated, nicely landscaped, and freshly painted. The cement front entry under the cantilevered overhang was about eight by fourteen feet, large enough for the nice intimate grouping of furniture they had carefully arranged. However, there was one glaring problem: The cement floor of the entry was covered with multicolored paint splatters.

"What happened here, Susan?" I asked the homeowner.

"Well," she offered, "when we were preparing the house to sell, the painters mixed all the paint here in the portico area."

"It may have been convenient for them," I commented, "but I suspect it may be costing you the sale of your home. This messy drop cloth of a floor is sending the wrong message. It simply does not fit the expectations buyers have of homes in your price range."

"You know, I wondered about that, but I decided I was making too much of a small thing," the homeowner replied.

"The sale is in the details," I said. "How would you like to learn a new craft?"

With a few sponges, a couple cans of paint, and a drop-cloth, I showed Susan how to stencil a running bond brick pattern over her unsightly cement porch floor. She transformed her liability into an asset and her sale sign into a sold sign. **The sale is in the details***. Unfortunately, like Violet and Red, she'd already had to lower the sale price.*

My experience has been that almost every home needs some tweaking before it's market ready. Even those homes that seem perfect, as if Martha Stewart herself had a hand in the smallest details, all need *something*.

5

Quick Sale Key

If buyers can't *see* the space,
they won't *buy* the space.

Hiding in Plain Sight

Neither the owners nor the agent had any idea why this beautiful, reasonably priced home wasn't selling. By the time they asked for my help the house had been on the market for over a year. As soon as I walked in the front door, I was pretty sure the answer lay at my feet.

The owners, Joe and Mary, were a friendly couple who had spent many years in Africa doing missionary work. Their home was traditional and tastefully decorated, with elegant hand-loomed rugs in every room. The rugs were not gaudy, brightly colored, or overwhelming in any way; it was simply that they were breathtakingly beautiful.

"Your home is lovely. The rugs are lovely. But I'd like to recommend that you remove every rug from your home before your next showing," I said.

"What?" Joe and Mary said in unison. I could see they were thunderstruck by my comment.

"I've never used her before," the real estate agent blurted out, being anxious to distance himself from my comments.

"But our rugs are so beautiful!"

"Yes, they really are," I agreed. "Let's move the rugs."

"But the rooms would be very dull without them."

"Yes, I think you're right. Let's move the rugs," I said.

"But the rugs are so precious to us. Each one of the rugs is filled with memories," Mary said.

"I understand. Now if you could just give me a hand with the rugs."

They muttered unmissionary-like comments under their breath as they moved the rugs—and showed me the door. Although I was certain I'd never hear from them again, the next day I received their call.

"Thank you, Diane," Mary said with excitement. "We sold the house to the first people who came through the house—after we moved the rugs.

Joe and Mary were very surprised. I was not. People are naturally drawn to what's most interesting. If the *things* in the house catch the eye and not the house itself, people don't see the house. And, I repeat, if they can't *see* the space, they won't *buy* the space.

The more things buyers have to look at, the more information they must retain to be able to evaluate the space. If you give them too much to remember, they end up with questions. Questions create doubt, and doubt often results in a lost sale.

6

Quick Sale Key

Neutral colors and design will improve your chances
for a fast and profitable sale
by appealing to more prospective buyers.

One Person's Treasure...

*Many people seem more interested in making a statement than in selling their home. One such home I visited was full of guns and taxidermy. Within that genre, Harley Hunter's home was well decorated, but I knew it would appeal to a small segment of potential buyers in the marketplace. **Anytime a home strongly reflects the personality and beliefs of the owner, it appeals to a much narrower percentage of the home-buying population.***

Even more troubling, the house came on the market during hunting season and that hard-to-find buyer was probably in the woods and would miss the open house.

"Harley, if you move some of the mounts and guns, then...."

Harley puttered around his desk and moved a box of bullets as I spoke. My gentle encouragement fell on deaf ears, so I cleared my throat and spoke up louder as I pulled out my own big guns.

"I'm surprised you want to market your home only to people who enjoy your hobbies."

That comment made Harley take notice of me and he sat down quietly. But I saw his eyes dart affectionately to Ben, his stuffed grizzly bear in the corner.

"If you want to market your home to such a small niche market, that's fine. However, you've hired me to help you sell your home quickly, and by attracting such a small market share, you radically reduce the chance of that happening. You should also know your decorating choice will probably cost you money in your sale price as well."

Well, my own big guns hit the mark because Harley and his wife had their hearts set on a hobby farm they'd found up north, so they decided to listen to me.

They removed the gun cabinet, all the stuffed animals and many of the wildlife paintings. Then they sent Ben on vacation. In just one hour, they were finished de-decorating. As is often the case, the most noticeable obstacles to selling a home can be eliminated very quickly and easily.

I called back a week later to see how they were doing. Harley and his wife were ecstatic; the house sold and they were packing Ben up for the trip to his new home on the hobby farm.

By neutral design, I mean not too much personality, not too much style, not too much color, not too much of any one ingredient. If there's a little something for everyone, but not enough of any one thing to turn people off, you increase the market base and your chance of selling quickly.

Houses are like ice cream. Some people like cinnamon ice cream, some people like rocky road, but almost everyone likes vanilla. I'm not criticizing your choice of cinnamon; I'm just saying if you want to sell more ice cream you're better off with vanilla.

7
Quick Sale Key

Make certain your home
holds no surprises for an unwary buyer.

Snakes, Monkeys and Lizards, Oh My!

One consultation that left a big impression on me was with a woman going through a painful divorce and very eager to sell her home.

As I walked through the house I wondered why I had been called to this home. It was immaculate, sparsely furnished (the husband had already taken his share), and each room had been freshly painted a desirably neutral shade of cream. I couldn't see any hindrances to a sale.

A big birdcage with several birds sat on the landing but having pets seemed a small thing—until I opened one of the bedroom doors. The room was filled with snakes. And I'm not talking about garter snakes either. In all fairness to the owner, many of them were in enormous glass aquariums, but there was at least one gigantic boa constrictor hanging from a dead tree. Did you see the movie Anaconda? Well, I didn't either. I hate snakes. It still makes my skin crawl to think about a bedroom crawling with them. All of a sudden the cage full of birds made sense. I guess the snakes liked the birds—for lunch.

It turns out that the woman was a belly dancer and used the snakes in her act. As my eyes darted from place to place and I fought the desire to stand on my chair rather than sit in it, I explained to her (from the point of view of a person who doesn't like snakes) why it was unlikely buyers would consider purchasing her home.

People wouldn't be thinking about making offers since they would be too busy wondering if any rogue snakes were lurking in the heat vents, ready with a big welcome hug for the new owners. She assured me that wasn't the case, and I assured her the facts were irrelevant. Fortunately, she had a partner in her act who agreed to take care of her cuddly friends until she moved into her new home.

I've never entered a house since without asking the owner if I could expect any surprises. I've encountered dogs as big as horses, flying cats, obscene birds, lizards, iguanas, snakes, rodents, and one demented feces-throwing monkey (at least I was ready to duck).

Not all surprises are as extreme as those I've encountered. However, a loose step, the only light switch located all the way across a dark basement, a closet door that falls off its track when opened, a door knob that comes off in your hand, water pipes that groan and sputter when you turn on a faucet, all can surprise and startle a prospective buyer. Surprised shoppers are uncomfortable shoppers, and uncomfortable shoppers are unlikely buyers. In conclusion, make sure there are *no* surprises.

8

Quick Sale Key

Eliminate reasons for buyers to make
negative assumptions about your home.

But, If I Could Just Explain

We had no plans to move from our home when I came home from a consultation, just ten days before our son Troy's wedding, and announced that I'd found a new home for us. The house was dated, very '50's—not my favorite design era, and it couldn't compare to our own home. But the back of the house was all glass and overlooked a beautiful, meandering creek on its way to the Mississippi River, complete with rapids and a small island.

We were hosting the groom's dinner at our home, and with rooms to paint, flowers to water and silver to polish, we were too busy to buy a house. But I wanted to live with that view and when I finally dragged my husband, Tom, to see it, so did he. We bought the house, fully confident our own home would sell to the first people who walked in the door, just like our last house had. After all, I'm a stager, right?

Before we could sell our home the city required us to disconnect our well and hook up to city water. I worried about digging up our park-like lawn we'd just redone for Troy's wedding, but when we talked to the contractor about the project he said, "No big deal, we only need a small trench to tap into the city water line." The trench would be long—about sixty feet, but only a foot wide, just twenty rolls of sod would cover it. No problem.

The morning of the great divide, as it came to be called, I was busy in my office doing final revisions on another book, when I thought to myself, "They sure have been digging a long time." I looked out the window at a hole so big the Grand Canyon paled in comparison. Racing out the door waving my arms like a crazy person I screamed, "Stop, you said only a small ditch!"

"Lady," he yelled back, "couldn't help it, soil's too dry. Get away from the edge, we don't have the equipment to go down and find you." Needless to say it took more than twenty rolls of sod to repair the damage.

We'd bought the creek house non-contingent, so we had no choice but to put our home on the market anyway. When our first buyers came to the house the yard looked more like a patchwork quilt than a lawn.

> *The disturbance in our yard raised all sorts of questions in the buyers' minds. But the very worst part was doing that digging around the water pipes caused them to burp unpleasant odors. We smelled it only once and it dispersed within a few minutes, but as luck would have it the pipes passed gas the first three times buyers came to the house. Not surprisingly, none of those first buyers bought the house. By the time we found out about the odor, the potential buyers had already moved to other homes and weren't interested in an explanation for flatulent pipes.*

I call this phenomenon the Iceberg Factor. When prospective buyers see obvious problems, it becomes easy for them to conclude they are only seeing *the tip of the iceberg* and that titanic problems lie below the surface.

Most of the time you don't get the opportunity to explain or answer questions, and, if you do, it's usually too late. The only recourse is to begin again with new buyers, a clean slate, and lots of antacid.

Whether you are making sure the house is ready for buyers when it's first listed, or you're eliminating reasons why buyers may make negative assumptions, your home must be in sync with the buyers' perceptions and expectations if you're looking for a quick sale in today's market.

**Remember—
The sellers are selling their *home*—
the buyers are buying a *house*.**

**How buyers *feel* is important because—
the more comfortable buyers feel in a house,
the more likely they are to buy it.**

Summary of
the Quick Sale Keys

When preparing your home for sale, make sure your home is
in peak selling condition *before* it goes on the market.

Make the improvements and changes
before you set your listing price.

Homes sell more easily if they fit well into the neighborhood.

The sale *is* in the details.

If buyers can't *see* the space, they won't *buy* the space.

Neutral colors and design will improve your chances
for a fast and profitable sale by appealing
to more prospective buyers.

Make certain your home holds no surprises
for an unwary buyer.

Eliminate reasons for buyers to make
negative assumptions about your home.

What do these keys all have in common? If your home meets
buyers' expectations in terms of quality, condition, cleanliness, and
perceived value, your home will sell faster, easier, and for more
money.

FIVE

Creating a Buyer-Friendly Environment with Space, Light and Color

It's important to understand the fundamentals of home staging before you begin to make changes. Recognizing the impact of the three basic design elements—space, light, and color—on the buyers' perception, will help you create the strongest visual presentation of your home because the

- **Space** affects the perception of the light and the color,
- **Light** affects the perception of the color and the space, and
- **Color** affects the perception of the space and the light.

When these elements work together, they produce a pleasing effect and create a buyer-friendly environment that make a sale more likely. When these elements are not in harmony, homes look less inviting and perspective buyers often respond with indifference, that *I can't put my finger on it* feeling, which makes them walk away.

If potential buyers feel a strong attraction to a house, they are likely to buy it—even if there are some things about the house they dislike. Their feelings override any concerns, and their desire to buy motivates them to think of changes they can make that would work for them. But if there is a lack of interest, that is the end of the story. *Indifference is the single biggest reason people don't buy—and homes don't sell.*

Even though opinions differ about what creates the ambiance that makes a buyer fall in love with a particular house, a number of principles hold true when dealing with space, light, and color. Using these principles to your advantage will help you overcome the obstacle of indifference and may just be the thing that captures your buyer's heart.

Element 1: Space

Space is your most valuable asset. It is what the seller is selling and the buyer is buying.

Even if you are moving from your home because you do not have enough space, it is important to create the perception of spaciousness. The smallest home can appear spacious, if arranged and organized properly.

The advantage of a well organized and arranged home is what I call spatial clarity. Spatial clarity is the ability to view and assess the space accurately. The more easily a buyer can assess and remember your home, the more likely they are to buy it.

What You See Is...What You See

One of the best examples of the importance of spatial clarity is a house I visited at the beginning of my staging career. I owned a floral business at the time and a real estate friend of mine called and asked if I had any extra flower arrangements he could borrow for one of his listings. Although I had nothing available to give him, I agreed to look at the house out of friendship.

As we drove to the house, I asked him about the circumstances of the move. Jack told me that the couple who owned the house were divorcing. The wife moved out over a year ago and took her half of their property with her. The house had been on the market since then and had lots of first showings, but so far no one expressed enough interest to return.

What Jack didn't tell me, but was immediately apparent on entering the front door, was the husband never rearranged the rooms to account for the missing pieces of furniture. In the living room, matching table lamps sat on the floor at either end of the sofa where end tables used to be. What had once been an arrangement of comfortable chairs near the TV at the far end of the living room now had one lone chair facing the empty TV cart.

The dining room had eight chairs sitting around an empty space. Call me psychic, but I'm guessing she took the table. The master bedroom still had a king-size bed and nightstands, but they were squeezed onto a short wall while the long wall that once must have held a large dresser stood empty. Each room looked more pathetic than the last.

I told Jack that I thought the problem was not the lack of decoration but lack of spatial clarity. Potential buyers were so confused by the furniture arrangement that they never got a fix on the space.

Fortunately, the unused lower level held some furniture we could use upstairs. We began moving things around and in a couple of hours the house looked better and offered—you guessed it—spatial clarity.

The home sold in less than a week. That simple favor for a friend helped me realize that even subtle changes could make a big difference in the sales process and gave me the confidence to launch my own home staging business.

Arranging Your Furniture

Openness and spatial clarity can be attained by making certain that nothing obstructs traffic patterns through the rooms. For example, you may be used to walking around the trunk at the end of the bed, but that arrangement could alter a person's perception of the available space in the room. Potential buyers may remember walking around the bed but not necessarily remember there was a trunk at the end of the bed. If they don't remember the trunk, they're left with the impression of a smaller bedroom. It's not that buyers can't tell the difference between a bed and a trunk; it's that every detail doesn't register accurately for most people on their first visit to a home—just the feelings remain.

Here's another example. Two things can occur when a bookcase that acts as a divider in the dining room is mistaken for a built-in feature rather than a placement choice. Buyers may desire a more open floor plan, or they may feel disappointed that the bookcase they thought was an architectural feature of the house is actually leaving with the owner. Either way you're better off removing the bookcase.

Famous architect Mies van der Rohe said "less is better and less is more." That classic design statement is certainly true when your home is for sale. Keeping the traffic patterns uncomplicated makes the space easier to remember. **The more buyers remember about a house the more likely they are to consider buying it.**

Conversely, the more cluttered and congested a home is, the more questions they have and the less likely they are to consider it. It's simply easier to move on than to search out answers about a home they may or may not be interested in.

You may end up needing to eliminate some pieces of furniture to open up the traffic flow through the room. If you have large furniture in small rooms, keep only the essential pieces. One of my own favorite rooms is a 10' x 10' guest bedroom with a queen-size bed and a nightstand—simple, yet elegant.

Quick Tip

If the size of your room necessitates minimum furnishings, but feels too bare after removing some of the furniture, hanging a picture on the wall will help dispel the emptiness.

If you have small furniture in a large room, do not spread it out to attempt to fill all the wall space. Instead, place the pieces into smaller conversational groupings, so the scale of the furniture remains in proportion to the floor area it occupies. Conversational groupings are arrangements where the distance between the chairs and the other furniture in the grouping is comfortable for both conversation and eye contact.

Quick Tip

Rooms will appear less cluttered and more open if you leave spaces between conversational groupings so there is an expanse of wall space visible from floor to ceiling.

To enhance the illusion of spaciousness, make sure the room feels balanced. One way to give the illusion of balanced space is to raise the visual height of the room if it has strong horizontal lines, or extend the visual width of the room if it has a tall or narrow aspect.

For example, vertically striped wallpaper, long narrow artwork, or floor length drapes can all add extra height to a room that feels vertically challenged. On the other hand, a valance above a window, horizontal blinds, or a row of pictures hung side-by-side above a low piece of furniture such as a desk could nicely square up a tall, but small, space.

The walls and floors of stairwell landings should be kept as open as possible. Already congested by nature of their limited space, these areas are likely places where your buyer could misstep, knock an unruly broom off the stairwell wall, or have a sale-breaking accident. Also, make sure the railings are securely attached. If a buyer feels safe in your home, it increases your chance for a sale.

Sometimes, just making sure a piece of furniture hugs the wall as much as possible can add a couple inches of valuable floor space, leaving a wider path between the sofa and chair, or the chest and bed. People often leave space behind a sofa or chair so the wall paint does not get marred, but when you're trying to sell your home, space is more important than paint.

Quick Tip

Attach self-adhesive bumpers or Velcro to the back of furniture to protect the walls from scuffs.

You can also make a room look more spacious by moving the largest pieces of furniture as far away from the doorway as possible. This use of perspective, keeping the smaller things closer and the larger pieces farther away, creates an illusion of depth and space that makes a room look larger and less crowded.

In rooms where every inch is important, placing a piece of furniture—a chair, small sofa, or dresser at an angle in a corner, can give you a bit of extra room. Rather than taking up more space, placing a piece of furniture at an angle creates the illusion of taking up less space because it uses part of two walls rather than one entire wall. In addition, a piece of furniture at an angle can help correct an awkward traffic pattern.

Figure 5-1

With the chest parallel to the walls, it appears to just fit. This placement also makes the side of the dresser visible, increasing its bulkiness and creating a narrow hallway when the door is open. Large accessories crowd the top of the dresser.

Placed at an angle, with wall space visible on both walls, the chest appears smaller and the *hallway effect* is eliminated. The space also feels more open with only one accessory, placed away from traffic, on the top of the chest.

Walking through the house to see if some furnishings might work better in different rooms can open your mind to the possibility of using things in new ways. Is it possible the sofa table, which causes you traffic problems in the living room, would work well as a bookshelf/ headboard in the bedroom, or as a sideboard in the dining room? Or maybe you could use one of the two nightstands in your bedroom as an end table in the living room.

In opening up the traffic pattern, remove anything on or near the wall next to a doorway. This is especially true if the item is dark-colored or juts out from the wall—such as a wall sconce, clothes hook, small shelf, or floor lamp. Just like an obstacle one would have to walk around, a dark or protruding object next to a doorway forces the eye to move around the object to see the space. This creates a closed-in feeling and cuts up the space visually. Keeping the area free of visual clutter allows the eye to travel more easily through the room and invites buyers into the space.

Figure 5-2

Notice how your view of the living room is impeded by the position of the floor lamp.

By eliminating the floor lamp and large plant, your eye is drawn to the longest sight line in the space, making the room seem larger.

Another great reason to keep doorways clutter-free is because prospective buyers often linger there. The longer they linger, the more likely they will buy, so give them plenty of elbow room in these areas.

The Stuff in Your Space

Most people have too much stuff and not enough elbow room. If the house isn't for sale, it's not a problem. However, when a home is for sale, overcrowded rooms, cupboards, bookshelves, and clutter on surfaces such as tables, desks, dressers, counters, or vanity tops, is detrimental to a sale. And sometimes they're even dangerous—I'm a frequent victim of closet avalanches. Make sure your buyers are safe from your stuff—or the next door they open might be the exit!

You may be saying to yourself: "What difference does it make? I'm taking everything with me when I move." It makes a big difference. I know the cupboards, closets, and bookcases will be empty when the new owners move in, but if these areas are full for showings, all potential buyers see is the *stuff*, not the *space*.

Buyers don't care about what you're going to do; they care about what they *see*. They *see* the clutter on the kitchen counter, the books piled in the bookcase, and the stack of mail on the desk so precariously perched that even the slightest touch could send it tumbling.

Figure 5-3

Notice how the kitchen clutter grabs your attention.

After eliminating the clutter, your eye is naturally drawn to the windows—the longest sight line.

Most of us live with a pile of unopened mail, cluttered countertops, and too many books in the bookcase. That's normal. Unfortunately *normal* doesn't sell houses and normal looks lousy in pictures on an Internet real estate site.

Clutter is public enemy number one. When a home has too much stuff, the distraction of visual clutter makes it hard for people to see anything else. Many potential buyers find it difficult, even impossible, to see the potential hidden beneath the stuff. The home's real value is too much work to assess and today's buyers leave without a backward glance because there are so many other houses for sale.

My clients often ask me, "What should I do with all my stuff?" Unfortunately, there's only one acceptable answer. "You can store it, sell it, or give it away, but you can't leave it out for buyers to see—if you want to sell your home quickly and for top dollar."

Every area needs to look clean, uncluttered, and well-organized for buyers to see its potential. *Every* closet, cupboard, shelf, and bookcase should appear only partially full.

It's easiest to begin by eliminating any furnishings, clothing, appliances, tools, etc., you are not taking with you. Don't let anyone think you are moving because you don't have enough room, even if that is the case. Removing non-essentials also gives you room to work and a head start on creating space.

Bookshelves, both built-in and free-standing, should be partially empty as well, with enough space for a new owner's special set of antique books. Each shelf should be no more than two-thirds full. If bookcases are completely full, then the visual wall of the room starts at the front edge of the bookcase, at the books' spines. On the other hand, if the bookcase is partially empty, then the visual wall recedes to the back of the bookcase, making the room seem larger.

Quick Tips

When removing books from your bookshelves, pack away the least attractive books and keep those books with the spines and cover colors that coordinate best with your decor.

Figure 5-4

With the bookcase entirely full, this feature is busy, uninteresting, and one dimensional.

By removing some of the books to reveal the back wall, the room seems larger. The variety also makes it easier for the buyer to imagine other ways to use these built-in shelves.

Maybe your buyers read little more than the daily newspaper and an occasional magazine, so they're not likely to be interested in bookcases. Use a picture, a knick-knack, a rock, a shell, or a small, healthy plant on some of the shelves to create the impression a bookcase has other uses. Having a few decorative items on the bookcase could help them see the space is just perfect for their collection of duck decoys, family photographs, collector plates, or shells.

In cupboards with glass doors, where the contents are visible, it's important that things appear well placed, orderly, and attractive, leaving ample room for the potential buyer to visualize Aunt Minnie's favorite plate or Grandma's antique teapot.

Quick Tip

When arranging items in a glass-fronted cupboards, put the white and clear glass objects in the front to increase the sparkle factor.

I'm frequently asked about closets. The same rules apply to closets as to every space. Make sure they are partially empty so potential buyers can see some unused shelf, hanger, and floor space in every closet.

Figure 5-5

See how crowded this closet looked before the owners thinned out their belongings. There is no room on the clothes rod, the shelves, or the floor for anything else.

By removing a few coats from the rod, hanging longer coats in the corners, and freeing some shelf and floor space, the closet appears to offer more room. With the back wall visible, the space seems larger and less crowded.

> **Quick Tip**
> Closets look their best when all the hangers are the same and all the clothes are hanging in the same direction.

De-clutter and evaluate all surfaces, not just the built-in bookcases or buffets that would be sold with the house. I mean *all* horizontal surfaces. From end tables to vanity tops, every surface needs space for whatever the new owners consider a necessity, whether that's a boom box or bath beads. Buyers want to know the house has room for the things *they* consider important.

There should be *no* toys in the bookcase, *no* tools in the kitchen cupboards, and *no* cans of paint in the bedroom closets. Remember the old saying: *A place for everything and everything in its place?* If things aren't where they belong, people jump to the conclusion there is not enough room to put them where they *do* belong—and buyers move along.

Pile storage boxes to the ceiling if need be, but limit their impact by keeping them all in the same place out of traffic patterns, in the farthest corner of your home—preferably the basement, garage, or attic. That way potential buyers have to see the boxes only once. It's seeing them everywhere that is so distracting. It might be necessary to rent some storage space or impose on the good will of a friend or family member who has space to spare, but if you want to sell your home in today's competitive market, you really have no choice.

Creating Additional Spacemakers

- **Take down curtains in small rooms to open up the space.**
  Removing all the window dressings adds light to a room and makes the area feel larger as well, especially in a room with a view where the drama of the room extends past the walls.

Quick Tip

If possible, remove the curtains entirely or just leave a valance with a window shade. If you want to keep your windows covered, consider replacing your curtains with mini-blinds or pleated shades. They require less space and don't make much of a design statement.

• **Create more walking space in a small dining room by removing any extra leaves and chairs from the table.**

Captain's chairs are larger and take a lot of space if the arms do not fit completely under the table. If this is the case, use side chairs instead, removing the larger chairs completely, or placing them at angles in the far corners of the dining room.

Figure 5-6

Before the captain's chair was moved from the end of the table, it was necessary to jog around the chair to open the patio doors. Potential buyers might have thought the space was inadequate.

After replacing the captain's chair with a side chair that slides completely under the table, there is ample room to exit the patio door, eliminating the traffic problem.

- **Paint every room the same color to create spaciousness and harmony.**

  As well as being both a color and light suggestion, painting the interior of your home the same neutral color creates a sense of flow that suggests the space is larger. I recommend a color like cream or eggshell rather than plain white, because these tones appear softer and don't produce as much glare in daylight.

- **Use the tops of any closets, cupboards, or ledges for display only.**

  If you want to have something on top of these surfaces, it should be purely decorative so buyers don't think the house is short on storage. Group display items at the far end of the surface so the feature is noticed; then leave the rest of the space empty. This approach draws attention to a closet, cupboard, or ledge rather than to what is on it.

- **Keep hooks on walls and on the backs of doors empty.**
  Most items placed on hooks intrude too much into the space and prevent the door from opening completely, making the doorway feel smaller and detracting from the room.

- **Adjust low-hanging light fixtures so buyers won't bump into them.**
  You may be used to ducking, but if perspective buyers hit their heads, they may also hit the road.

- **Create the illusion of more space with mirrors.**
  Just as mirrors increase the amount of available light in a room, they also give the perception of more space. To increase the size of the room, hang a mirror opposite the doorway. To make an even greater impact, use a mirror over the mantel of a fireplace to draw more attention to the room's focal point.

- **Remove any mobiles or hanging plants.**
  They require too much visual space.

De-decorating Your Beautiful Spaces

Sometimes, even after owners have removed the optional furniture and extra *stuff*, the rooms still look so beautifully furnished and accessorized, it's difficult for buyers to visualize the space furnished with their own things. In these cases, dressing down and de-decorating the rooms becomes necessary.

When you're selling, it's time to put the focus back where it needs to be—on the space itself.

Window coverings and accessories make a room look *put together* and instill it with the owner's energy and personality—the very thing you want to avoid when your house is for sale. By simplifying window treatments and removing accessories, you remove some of the room's personality and make way for the personality of the potential buyer.

Figure 5-7

Although tastefully decorated, the throw on the sofa, the vase of sunflowers, the pottery turtle underneath the table, and the other accessories grab all your attention.

A little de-decorating gives potential buyers a better chance to see the space. Notice how your eye moves to the chiminea lamp in the far right corner instead of towards the sofa as in the previous picture.

An accessory can be almost anything—a teddy bear or a bronze sculpture, a sailboat or a ceramic animal, a lamp made from a milk can, a bowl of apples, a vase full of flowers, a pile of books, a birdhouse, or a collection of who knows what.

Glance through any decorating magazine and you'll quickly see what I mean. If you take another look you'll notice nearly every surface is filled with these wonderful things. They look great. They are the jewels in the crown of decorating. The only time this becomes a problem is when the house is for sale, because these great displays do *exactly* what they are intended to do. They attract all the attention. This is fine when the boss and his wife are coming to dinner, but *not* when you want to sell the house. Begin to de-decorate by removing the accessories that:

- **Possess the most color or pattern**—they attract too much attention.

- **Hold a special place in your heart**—When your grandmother's antique chandelier becomes the negotiating item between you and the buyers, things can get messy. Remove the item and eliminate the issue.

- **Occupy the most space** (particularly *floor space*)—if you don't need it, it shouldn't be there making the room seem smaller.

- **Cost the most money**—there is no reason to risk having a precious possession get broken, or intimidate a possible buyer with the cost of your belongings.

- **Make the most personal statements about you**—your beliefs, your interests, your hobbies, your passions, your taste.

Figure 5-8

Although this room is very attractive in person, the style is too busy for a small Internet picture—the way 86 percent of buyers find their home before scheduling a showing.

After removing a large plant to provide bare wall space, the pillows, throw, and some accessories from the tables and hearth, the room is much easier to absorb.

After removing the most obvious accessories, survey your room for anything that you could do without, especially if the room is small and it occupies floor space such as

- a magazine rack
- a set of fireplace tools
- an umbrella stand
- a coat rack
- a footstool
- baskets—empty or full
- floor pillows
- a vase full of dried or silk flowers (particularly if it sits on the floor)
- knick-knacks
- collections of any kind—dolls, plates, salt and pepper shakers, figurines, knives. You name it—I've seen the collection.

Figure 5-9

With the winter village on the mantel, you notice the village, not the fireplace.

With the village removed, the focus is on the fireplace—a valuable selling feature.

Though it's not possible to name every accessory, I'm confident if you spend even a short time surveying the contents of any room, it will become readily apparent what you need to put away—*the very things that make the room yours.*

Once the accessories have been removed, you can reintroduce some interest by re-accessorizing your rooms following these principles:

- **Every item matters.**

  Everything that doesn't add—detracts. If your beautiful vase is sitting next to an assortment of dog-eared magazines or dying plants, the vase's impact is wasted.

- **Use no more than three items on any surface.**

  An odd number is always more interesting to the eye and feels more complete. If the surface is very large, such as a sideboard, you may use as many as five items, but only one large surface per room. Keep it simple.

- **Vary the heights of the objects.**

  Varying the heights helps the eye move effortlessly through the space.

- **Vary the mass of the objects.**

  A variety of sizes helps the arrangement work more proportionately in the space.

- **Vary the textures of the objects.**

  Varying the textures creates a feeling of warmth and comfort.

- **Provide a unifying characteristic among the objects on a surface.**

  A sense of unity creates a peaceful, quieting atmosphere, which raises people's comfort level. The unifying quality could be the same or similar color, shape, or theme.

De-decorating and re-accessorizing in an impersonal way can be difficult, but this step is the key to creating an environment where potential buyers can imagine your home as theirs. Hang in there, you're doing great!

Using Your Walls to Enhance the Space

Artwork is an integral part of accessorizing a home, and reveals a lot about its owners. When selling your home, art should enhance the beauty of your home rather than create controversy. Choosing subject matter such as landscapes, still lifes, flowers, birds, or architecture is safe and has general appeal.

All your artwork should fit easily onto the wall space, with room to spare. If it just fits the space, with very little wall left over, buyers may remember the size of the wall by the size of the picture. For example, a buyer might say, "I don't think the dining area was very big because there was only enough room for one picture on the wall."

Figure 5-10

This picture fits too closely in the available room, making the picture size disproportionate to the wall.

With a smaller, narrower picture, more in proportion to the wall, the space feels open, the wall larger.

This perception problem can be avoided if you make sure each picture has a substantial border of wall space around it. The negative space has the additional advantage of allowing buyers to use their imagination to fill the wall space with their own things.

If you have artwork in hallways, hang it only on one side of the hall to prevent buyers from feeling claustrophobic. Leave at least one wall unadorned in each room to enhance the feeling of spaciousness and potential.

One note of caution: Don't hang anything too close to a doorway. This makes the entry area of the room feel less open. Objects are also more likely to get bumped or damaged near an entry path—making you unhappy and the potential home buyer uncomfortable.

Although the basic message of this book is "less is more," a limited amount of artwork on your walls is a good thing. It provides some interest and keeps the potential buyer's eyes moving smoothly throughout the rooms.

The rules for hanging wall art are many, and meant to be creatively broken. Keeping that in mind, a few simple tips can help anyone achieve a more desirable effect.

- **Keeping Things Symmetrical**

  Most people feel comfortable when rooms are arranged symmetrically. The basics of that statement are easy to grasp. If you place a tall candleholder on one side of the mantel, most people find it pleasing to have a similar candleholder on the other side of the mantel.

  This holds true for anything hanging on a wall. If you place a large painting over the center of the sofa, you can put a smaller one on each side. You can also put the small ones on top of each other on one side of the large painting, but only if you have centered the entire arrangement over the sofa. Think of it this way—an arrangement of wall art is like a teeter-totter. You need to have a center of balance.

- **Creating Balance**

  When creating balance with your accessories, note that dark-colored wall accessories appear heavier than light-colored accessories. You can compensate by having more light than dark pieces, if there is a variety in the color of the accessories. Big accessories also appear to weigh more than small pieces, so the same principles apply.

- **Using a Common Element**

  A common element can tie together dissimilar pieces. You can use several photographs of different subjects, but if they are all framed alike they become one unified piece of art. Similarly, you can have several pictures of the same subject and create a single theme.

  Other unifying elements besides the framing or subject could be the matting, shape, or color. When hanging a photo gallery, you can achieve a more pleasing composition if all the pictures are framed similarly and are either all color photos or all black and white photos.

- **Hanging Art at the Correct Height**

  Generally speaking, when there's nothing under the picture, such as a table, desk, chair, bed, or sofa, the best height to hang a picture is so the center of the picture is about 62–64 inches from the floor.

  If a picture or arrangement is hanging above another object, it looks best if the bottom of the picture and the top of the other element (i.e., the table, desk, chair, bed, or sofa, etc.) are separated by no more than about 6–12 inches. The picture, arrangement, or collage should be centered above, and be no longer than the piece of furniture below it.

When putting together different pieces of wall art to create a collage, remember the outside of the arrangement should form a geometric shape, such as a square, rectangle, or a circle.

It's important for all the design elements to relate to each other, and grouping them closely helps the room hang together.

When your home is for sale, use art sparingly to make your property (and not your furnishings) the center of attention.

Your home may seem empty and less interesting to you after removing some furnishings and accessories, but keep in mind, it won't feel bare to someone who hasn't been there before. Fewer furnishings and accessories will provide your buyers with spatial clarity. **Your goal is to help the buyer see the space, not the contents.**

Element 2: Light

Generally speaking, people like new surroundings to be filled with as much natural light as possible. Even people who tend to close the drapes and pull the blinds in their own space, prefer new spaces to be well lit. Light has the ability to make a small space appear larger, a drab space brighter, a boring space more interesting, and a new space more welcoming.

Good light makes a house feel safer and puts people at ease, both factors are critical to a sale. It just makes sense that if someone is comfortable in your home, they are much more likely to buy it.

Making a buyer feel *at home* can also reduce the natural stress of shopping for a new home. A relaxed buyer is a more ready buyer. So open the blinds, and let the light in!

When It Rains, It Pours

I've known for a long time that light has a powerful effect on the way a space is perceived, but when putting our own home on the market even I was surprised by the difference light made.

After my husband, Tom (a Realtor® himself) and I finished the initial preparations to sell our home, we invited several of our real estate friends to come over for a wine and cheese party to help us set a listing price. Tom had already done a comparative market analysis, but because we knew we were biased, we thought additional advice would be helpful.

It was a sunny, warm, summer day when about half the group arrived. After giving them a tour of the house, we asked them to fill out a questionnaire and give us their expert opinion about the price—anonymously, of course.

The rest of the agents came about an hour and a half later. By this time, it clouded up, and began to rain. We gave them the same tour of the house, plied them with food and drink, and asked them to fill out the same questionnaire.

Later when we compared the prices, the first group averaged about $50,000 higher than the second group. We were stunned! We began to try to figure out what could have made such a big difference. In the end, we realized the only difference between the first and second groups' experience was the weather and how it impacted the light both inside and outside our home.

Make it a priority to increase both your natural and artificial light—it can make a considerable difference in the perceived value of your house.

Natural Light

Windows are your most valuable source of natural light. Take advantage of them whenever you can by leaving your drapes and curtains open. The natural light in the room playing off window glass will make the space appear more interesting to prospective buyers, whether they're on the outside looking in or on the inside looking out.

Make sure your curtains and drapes cover as little of the window glass as possible. Using tiebacks will reveal more glass and minimize the volume of the window coverings as well as increase the light penetration into the room.

If you have both sheers and drapes, consider removing one pair to increase the light. The light effect will be even more dramatic if you remove the window coverings completely. At first glance, some homeowners resist this idea because they think the room will look unfinished without window coverings. Although it may take some getting used to for the owner, nothing will be missing for the buyer.

Quick Tip
You can make tiebacks easily by using ribbons, scarves, or corded tassels, and attaching them to cup hooks secured to the wall.

Removing just the valance or cornice board can lighten the surroundings and visually lift the ceiling as well. Or you can take the opposite approach by removing the curtains and leaving only the cornice board or valance. This approach not only adds more light to the room but the strong horizontal line also extends the width of the wall.

Quick Tip
If you have light-colored blinds, keep them down but open. This position allows them to be noticed and also provides the most light. Dark-colored blinds should be pulled all the way up to keep them from draining light from the room.

If your windows are in poor condition or have fogged over like so many casement windows tend to do, cover them with white or cream lace curtains. They minimize the problem while still letting in light.

Remember, when your home is on the market, it's for sale twenty-four hours a day. Your buyers may drive by anytime as they consider the purchase of your home.

Artificial Light

Even on a sunny day, most homes require some artificial lighting to show them to their best advantage. Whether you use ambient lighting, task lighting, or accent lighting depends on the effect you wish to create.

- **Ambient lighting** is the general light we use to illuminate our indoor spaces. These lights are usually in the ceiling and provide all over illumination.

- **Task lighting** is used to light areas for specific tasks such as under cabinet lighting in the kitchen, desk lamps, table lamps, chandeliers, or wall sconces.

- **Accent lighting** or spot lighting can be used to illuminate something such as a painting, a fireplace wall, or other architectural feature. Both task and accent lighting produce more than just light. By generating uneven light and shadows, spot lighting creates contrasts that add to the mood, texture, and interest of a room.

When selling your home, while it's important to have sufficient general illumination, it is the accent and task lighting that make your home look more interesting. Have you ever noticed how much more appealing and interesting restaurants look when they use fewer ceiling lights and more light either directly over or on each table? This is because overhead lighting or light above eye level makes a space seem cooler, more industrial, and less personal, while light at eye level or below seems warmer and more personal. Your home will appear *warmer* and friendlier for evening showings if you use table lamps and accent lighting in addition to your *cool* ceiling lights.

You may need to buy a few lamps to make sure buyers have enough light to be comfortable in your home and to create a warm and inviting mood.

Quick Tip

A good way to determine if you have enough light is to check in the evening to see if you need to be near a lamp to read a newspaper.

If you do, it's probably a good idea to add more light. Most people need about 40 percent more light at age forty than they do in their twenties. It's better to have too much light than too little. Small lamps can be inexpensively purchased at any discount store, and may be just what you need to create a cozy nook out of a dark corner.

To add light in a room with a ceiling fan, one option might be to purchase a light for the fan. Fan lights are inexpensive, easy to install, and available at any home improvement store.

You can create interest as well as light, by using an inexpensive spotlight to backlight a floor plant. Accent lighting is especially effective in bedrooms and living rooms where a warmer, more inviting mood is an advantage.

Quick Tip

While a chandelier is often hung low to provide the best light, raising it can help people get a better look at what is beyond the chandelier, such as a built-in buffet, a bay window, a wonderful view, or a long sight line through to another room. However, if the chandelier is the best feature in sight, hang it so it will dominate the space.

You can increase the appeal of any bathroom with a vanity countertop by adding a small lamp. It will dispel the sterile look common in so many bathrooms and create a warmer, more pleasing appearance. Adjusting the height of bathroom swag lights so they reflect in the mirror can also provide additional light where you need it.

Figure 5-11

In this picture, all the light comes from an overhead source. Notice how every surface has the same tonal value and looks flat.

See how the lamp light makes the space more interesting by providing a warm pool of light—a different tonal quality.

It's especially important to leave lights on even during the day where there is little or no natural light, or where a real estate agent or buyer might find the switch difficult to locate, such as basements, closets, laundries, and bathrooms.

Replace any old, mismatched light plates. Broken dirty covers send negative messages. Why take the risk when, for about a quarter a switch, you can send a positive one instead?

Adding a dimmer switch is an inexpensive amenity, and it allows you to control the lighting in your rooms, depending on the time of day and the mood you wish to create. You also can increase the light by:

- **Painting dingy ceilings to reflect more light into your space.**
  Giving ceilings a fresh coat of white paint is relatively inexpensive and makes a remarkable difference in the quality of light.

- **Adding accessories in soft neutral tones and reflective metal finishes.**
  Even rooms with darker colors in the carpet, sofa, drapes, or bedspread can seem lighter when you dilute the color with reflective metal or light-colored accessories.

- **Hanging mirrors.**
  Place a mirror across from a window to reflect outside light and create the effect of another window.

- **Clearing objects from the windows and windowsills.**
  Remove all suncatchers, wind chimes, mobiles, hanging plants, and anything else hanging in the window that limits the natural light. If something reduces the natural light, it also blocks the view.

- **Moving furniture that blocks any portion of a window.**
  Just moving a lamp and table away from the front of the picture window can be a big help to increasing the light in a room.

- **Preventing your artwork from stealing valuable light from your room.**

  Oil paintings or dark-colored wall hangings absorb light. Replace your light-absorbing artwork with pictures that are covered with glass in the framing to reflect light back into the room. Similarly, pictures that use light colors and have metal or gold frames appear lighter and are preferable to dark wood frames.

- **Making sure your windows allow the maximum amount of light to enter your home.**

  Dirt accumulates on windows daily from wind and weather, and this film reduces the amount of light that enters the windows. Making sure your windows are sparkling clean will help your buyers see clearly.

- **Removing your window screens in the winter to let in more light.**

  Removing window screens during the colder months brings in more light and draws in additional heat as well.

- **Using the highest watt bulbs in your light fixtures.**

  Higher wattage bulbs will ensure that each space looks its best and brightest. If your home is north-facing or deficient in natural light, use full-spectrum bulbs to create the effect of natural light in your home.

- **Scheduling your showings during the day.**

  Whenever possible, suggest showing times when the light is most flattering to your home.

Several years ago, we remodeled our home by adding a wall of windows in the living room and opening up the wall between the living room and kitchen. After the remodeling was complete, we noticed that nearly everyone who came to our home commented on our addition. When we told people that we had not added any square footage, they were always very surprised. The room remained the same size, but the increased light and expanded view magnified the space so dramatically everyone thought our home was actually larger. It also got rid of my winter blues. Let there be light!

Element 3: Color

Today's color trends can offer a challenge when selling your home because **color is a very personal issue**. One person's dream of a purple bedroom is another person's nightmare. Wherever color is present, there is going to be someone who does not like that color, and every time you add another color, you further reduce the chances that potential buyers will like all your color choices.

When neutral colors are used, no one is going to walk in and say their furniture doesn't work in a room with cream walls. However, it's very possible someone might come in and say that their blue and mauve sofa would not look good in an olive green living room. With neutral colors, color is eliminated as a reason to reject a home.

It's Not Easy Being Green, or Violet, or...

When the agent told me the home she wanted me to visit was owned by two designers, I knew I had my work cut out for me. I was right. The entry way was violet, the living room a deep olive green, and the dining room a dark terra cotta. Unlike the Red and Violet Hughes home, it was beautiful and elegant, but I also thought it was going to be a tough sale.

I explained to them that potential buyers needed to like violet as soon as they walked in the door, then they needed to like both violet and deep olive green as they entered the living room, and as they moved into the dining room they needed to like violet, deep olive green, and dark terra cotta. They were limiting the potential buyers to only those people who shared their taste.

> *Explained that way, they were very receptive to making changes and the agent told me they painted the entry way before the end of the day.*

It's very simple: The more colors you have, the more you reduce the odds of finding a buyer who likes those same colors. To sell your home in a buyers' market, you want your home to appeal to the largest number of potential buyers, so neutralize color as much as possible.

Neutralizing the Color in Your Home

Bold wall colors have a strong visual impact. Because walls possess the most surface space in a room, when they are painted with bold colors they capture more attention than anything else. A large expanse of color can keep people from being able to focus on the features of your home. In most cases, you will appeal to more buyers and increase your home's salability by reducing the bold color elements in your home.

What do I mean by bold color? Not all bold colors are bright colors, but all bold colors are strong or intense. Forest green, burgundy, and chocolate brown are all examples of bold or intense colors but they are not considered bright colors.

One indicator of bold color is to notice where your eye goes first when you enter a room. Most often it will go to the strongest color. If your eye goes to a feature like a fireplace or a great view, it is less likely that color is a problem.

Quick Tip

My test for determining if a color is intense is to imagine it on a kitchen countertop. For example, although navy blue is not a bright color, if you imagine it on a countertop, it is bold and makes a strong statement.

The most obvious way to neutralize the color in your home is to remove brightly colored paint or wallpaper and repaint the walls. The lighter neutrals: beige, cream, off-white, or even taupe paint are the best color choices to use when repainting walls for market appeal. Do not use pure white paint except on the ceilings; on walls it looks harsh and like florescent light, is unflattering to skin tones.

When repainting, begin with the walls in the first boldly colored room that buyers will see when they enter your home, such as the entry or the living room. If a color turns a buyer off as soon as they walk in the door, it's pretty hard to undo that first impression. However, when a color issue is farther along on the tour of the house, it doesn't carry as much risk because the buyer may already be in love.

Quick Tip

Unlike the '80s and '90s when wallpaper ruled the design world, today it is being used sparingly, if at all. Just like with boldly colored walls, begin by removing the wallpaper in the front of the house such as the entry, foyer, or living room area where people form their first impression.

If you're not game to eliminate all your wallpaper, remove it where you can see more than one paper in a glance. For example, if you have three wallpapered rooms in a row, remove the wallpaper from the one in the middle; the visual break helps to keep the wallpaper issue from feeling overwhelming to a prospective buyer.

Like wallpaper, stained wood paneling is not currently popular and makes a room seem dark and dated. However, cream or off-white painted paneling is very trendy and looks fresher, and brighter. So consider painting your paneling, especially where it covers walls in your main living space.

Even if you don't reduce the color elsewhere in your home, consider painting the bedrooms, where a softer palette helps to create a quiet, restful environment. Bedrooms are very personal spaces and most people have definite feelings about the color they want surrounding them eight hours a night.

In addition to painting walls, an easy suggestion to reduce color in a bedroom is to reverse the bedspread. Even if it is not a reversible spread, the underside of the spread can still be preferable. You can also reduce the color by using white or cream sheets and leave the spread or coverlet neatly folded at the end of the bed.

In some rooms it may not be possible to remove the color because the "problem" is the sofa, carpet, or some other large item that you do not want to replace. In this case, you can reduce the impact of the color by making sure other items in the room do not provide dramatic contrast. For instance, a blue sofa with red and yellow plaid pillows makes a much stronger statement than the same sofa with tan and white plaid pillows.

You can create a more neutral palette in any room by eliminating brightly colored accessories, such as pillows, pictures, throws, rugs, books, or bedspreads.

You might think that the room looks less attractive without as much color, and that may be true. However, **this process is about showcasing the space, not the decorating**. The goal is to help the buyer see the space and not get stuck because they don't like green walls and you do.

Figure 5-12

In a small room with dark walls, keep things simple. It is easy to overwhelm the buyer and make the room seem even smaller with patterns, pillows, extra color, and a teddy bear.

With the print quilt turned over, the extra pillows and teddy bear removed, and a small arrangement added, your eye is drawn to the longest sight line in the left corner. When the picture above the bed is replaced with a smaller one that hangs vertically, the room appears larger. Although not as interesting, the space is more saleable.

Some *Color-less* Ideas

If the room appears uninteresting after you have removed the more colorful accessories, try some color-less ideas by:

- Using brass or glass candlesticks and vases to add sparkle and pizzazz, without additional color.

- Adding texture with wood-toned baskets, stones, shells or *healthy* green plants in brass or unobtrusive containers.

- Softening the impact of large wood dining tables, chests or dressers with cream or white tablecloths to make them appear less imposing.

- Draping neutral-colored throws on boldly-colored sofas and chairs like slipcovers to reduce the expanse of color.

You can also use color psychology to your advantage when you are selling your home. Red is the first color people see in the spectrum. A red accent, properly placed, will draw a buyer's visual attention towards a feature or away from a flaw. Place the accessory near your home's feature to help them notice it, or at a distance from the flaw to draw their eye away and minimize it. For example, put red candles on the mantel to draw attention to the fireplace, and place a bouquet of red flowers on the table in front of the window with a poor view.

Whether you're raising blinds, moving furniture, or painting walls, understanding how the elements of space, light, and color affect potential buyers is essential to improving your home's salability quotient.

Some of the ideas presented are big, some are just tweaks. Most of the time, it is not just one change that makes the difference, but the total effect of a number of changes.

Together these changes give your home a fresher, cleaner, brighter look, making it feel more available and comfortable to prospective buyers and increasing your opportunity for a quicker sale and a better price.

SIX

Making Your Home Irresistible to Buyers

Now it's time to get down to specifics with my space-by-space appraisal. But before you begin, I want to share my **Three Simple Questions** and **Seven Staging Secrets** with you.

If you keep these three questions and seven secrets uppermost in your mind as you evaluate each room, you will be able to make your changes easily and with confidence.

Three Simple Questions

As you prepare each room, ask yourself the following questions:

One—Is there enough unused *space* in this room to allow potential buyers to move through it easily and without distraction?

Two—Is there enough *light* in this room to allow everyone to see clearly and feel comfortable?

Three—Does the room have enough neutral *color* to be acceptable to most people?

You may be thinking these questions are *so* simple they couldn't possibly make much difference—so simple that everyone must know them. You're right: These questions are so simple and straightforward that although they're not really a secret, they are easily overlooked.

Using the **Three Simple Questions** will help you create a more saleable house, one that will appeal to a larger share of the home-buying market and sell faster than others because there is enough:

- Open **space** so people can easily engage their imaginations and see your *house* as their *home*.

- Natural and artificial **light** for buyers to see the house clearly and feel comfortable.

- Neutral **color** so buyers won't be turned off.

Seven Staging Secrets

Along with the **Three Simple Questions**, using my **Seven Staging Secrets** will give you the insight you need to prepare your home to sell faster in any market.

1st Secret

You don't need the best decorated rooms;
you need rooms that appeal to the largest market share.

No matter what the current design trends are, fewer furnishings, better light, and less vibrant color all increase your home's sale potential. By making it easier for a buyer to imagine a room furnished differently, or used in other ways, you increase the number of buyers— and your chances for a sale.

2nd Secret

If you remove some of your belongings,
buyers are more inclined to buy.

Moving around some of your furniture and removing some of your things depersonalizes the space for *you* and your buyer. Your home will feel more like a house. This change in energy will make it easier for you to go—and for buyers to stay.

3rd Secret

Maximize the available space in your home.

Remove all non-essential furnishings, especially near the entryways to each room. If buyers linger, they often stand in doorways. Open entry areas facilitate good traffic flow and home-buying conversations.

4th Secret

Keep buyers' attention focused on the house
by reducing attractive distractions.

A focused buyer is in the right frame of mind to make a purchase. Too many books, wall hangings, collectibles, or furnishings, become a barrier between the buyer and the space. In other words, too much stuff not only creates an obstacle between your buyer and your home, but also between you and a sale.

5th Secret

Eliminate your personal scent from your home.

Every home has its own smell—the combination of the food, furnishings, cleaning products, and the people and pets that live there. The sense of smell registers consciously and unconsciously with almost everyone. Airing out your home every day for ten minutes, gives your entire home a fresh, clean smell that registers positively with buyers.

There are a few smells that everyone seems to like such as vanilla, cinnamon, and coffee. You can use vanilla or cinnamon extract on a small piece of aluminum foil on top of a light bulb (the heat from the bulb releases the scent) or you can make coffee. I have heard that coffee not only creates a friendly smell but also stimulates the buying impulse. It might be worth a try.

Do not use artificial air fresheners with fragrance. Many people are allergic to chemically reproduced smells and can have serious reactions when exposed to them. In addition, some people use strong scents to cover up undesirable odors. It's much better to eliminate the problem smell than cause visitors to wonder what you're covering up and why your home smells just like the bathroom at the gas station. If you need to remove an odor, use an odor neutralizer or eliminator instead.

6th Secret

Add dimension to your home with sound.

Like smell, sound also registers consciously and unconsciously with people. If a home is too quiet, it makes people feel uneasy (you can tell because they begin to whisper), and people don't buy homes where they feel uncomfortable.

Hearing the rustle of leaves in the trees or kids playing in the yard, makes people feel comfortable; so if outside sounds are pleasant, leave the windows open. If the sounds outside seem more like noise, then put on a CD or classical music station—*softly* please. Handel's "Water Music" is a good choice because it is both upbeat and calming.

7th Secret

Meet buyers' expectations.

The ad says "a view of the lake," but when buyers visit they discover the lake is only visible from the front corner of the west window in the bathroom.

Don't disappoint buyers. Be enthusiastic, embellish but don't exaggerate, and make sure the home's furnishings reflect the home's value. In a less expensive home, people expect owners to cut corners. In a more expensive home, buyers may wonder what other corners have been cut. As home values rise, so do expectations.

Finally, although not much of a secret, a clean home is still the most powerful magic you can have in your bag of home-selling tricks. Even in a fiercely competitive market like this one, the majority of homes for sale are not very clean. Having your home spotlessly clean may not make it the best house in the world, but it may make it the best house in your price range, which is even more important.

SEVEN

Improving Your Home's Curb Appeal

Whether online or in person, your potential buyers' first view of your property is the *outside space*. It is during the first few seconds buyers look at your home that they form their first impression, so it's important to catch their attention right away.

After all, if people don't like the outside of your home, there's a good chance they may not want to see the inside. Statistics indicate more than 80 percent of buyers know by the time they reach the front door whether they are interested.

Begin by taking a drive through your area to see how your home compares to the rest of the neighborhood. Don't hesitate to copy someone else's good idea. If it works for them, it's likely to work for you too. For example, if you find that homes similar to yours consistently look better with shutters or window boxes, you may want to consider adding them.

Then change the things you planned to change about the appearance of your house when you bought it, but learned to overlook. Competition is stiff. People are busier than ever, so what you considered a small problem when you bought your home, could be a much bigger obstacle to a sale today. Make the changes now, rather than risk losing potential buyers.

As a rule, I advocate spending as little money as possible when you're selling your home so you'll have it to spend on your new place. But if you do need to spend money, spend it where you will get the most return—out front improving your home's curb appeal because *first impressions are everything.*

Potential buyers are unpredictable. You can't possibly know exactly what will appeal to everyone. However, it's pretty easy to predict what could turn someone off immediately like:

- weed-filled cracks in the sidewalk

- a lawn with more weeds than grass

- house and trim colors that don't complement one another

- rust stains on the house or sidewalk from a leaky faucet

- weeds sprouting from debris-filled gutters

- torn screens on the door or windows

- outdoor light fixtures with broken glass, or *no* glass at all

Although the list is virtually endless, here are some musts to get you started.

The Exterior Space Checklist

- Determine whether your home looks best when approached from the right or the left side and include directions for approaching your house in the showing instructions.

- Check to see if your front door can stand up to the close scrutiny it will get from potential buyers as they wait for the real estate agent to open the door.

- Repair and repaint any shabby house or trim paint that may turn off buyers as they approach your front door.

- Keep all the curtains and shades hanging evenly in the windows so the house looks neat and orderly from the outside.

Figure 7-1

The uneven blinds draw negative attention right away and may cause potential buyers to make the assumption that the house is not well maintained.

With the blinds hanging straight, no one would jump to the conclusion the home has been neglected.

- If your house color is bold and you're not planning to paint the whole house, consider changing the trim color to something more neutral. Just changing the color of the front door or shutters can make a dramatic difference too. A blue house with cream trim is much softer than the same house with gold trim. By using similar paint colors and landscaping choices as your neighbors, your home will blend into the neighborhood.

- Clean out your gutters and downspouts.

- Reattach any loose shingles.

- Plant flowering bushes or shrubs with variegated foliage to brighten things up if your house is painted with dark colors or if the landscaping needs a facelift.

Quick Tip

Potentillas are inexpensive, hardy shrubs that bloom profusely from spring through fall in sunny locations. You can also place white or yellow flowering potted plants such as daisies, chrysanthemums, petunias, or impatiens among your other shrubbery.

- Mow your lawn, trim your shrubs, weed your gardens, and sweep your walkways to make a good first impression.

- Top fill any planting areas where the groundcover (i.e., rocks, bark, wood chips) does not completely cover the soil.

Quick Tip

In many areas, tree-trimming companies will deliver their scrap wood chips at no charge. Although the quality of the chips is less consistent than what you would purchase at a garden center, they look fine in most surroundings and the price is certainly right.

Many communities also offer free chips to their residents if you pick them up from their dumpsite. Five-gallon buckets work well to transport the chips. You can just scoop them up, load a number of buckets in the trunk and easily dump them into your gardens.

Figure 7-2

This close-up shows only a corner of the weedy garden that runs the entire length of the house. Its scraggly appearance made the entire backyard look messy and unkempt. Due to the limited on-street parking, this unsightly view greeted potential buyers before they reached the entry door.

It took less than three hours to weed the garden, cut in a new edge, and add a dozen buckets of wood chips. Now buyers are more likely to still be interested when they reach the door and sellers have a much better chance to attract buyers with a charming interior.

- Trim any foliage or plantings that impede the street view of the house.

- Be sure your walk, driveway, and deck are neatly shoveled or snow blown if you are selling in the winter.

- Avoid making footprints in a snowy front yard if you can since the winter landscape looks so much prettier without them.

- Remove any trees and/or shrubs that block windows or hang over the sidewalk, crowding the front door.

Figure 7-3

The owner of this house bought it twenty years ago because she thought it was so cute. When I pointed out that the front of the house was no longer visible she told me she hadn't even noticed. She held the beauty of her home in her heart and no longer saw how the overgrown arborvitaes spoiled the home's curb appeal.

Look at the amazing transformation that occurred when the arborvitaes were removed. Not only are the bushes gone but so are the long shadows that made the house so dark. This home is not just average—it is darling and buyers thought so too. It sold the first weekend in a bidding war.

- Keep your lawn fertilized and weed-free.
- Fill window boxes and planters with flowers and greens so they're viewed as an asset instead of a liability.

Quick Tip

If you don't wish to maintain live plants during the growing season, fill the containers with soil and cover them with sphagnum moss to create the look of possibilities and plant readiness. You could also place flower seed packets on small stakes in the boxes to engage the buyer's imagination.

During late fall and winter, spruce treetops are readily available at most nurseries and some grocery stores. They create seasonal beauty in window boxes and planters, and are maintenance-free. Adding twinkle lights dramatically heightens the effect during the darker winter months.

- Remove the weeds from any cracks in the sidewalk or driveway.
- Make sure the sidewalk and front steps look their best.

Quick Tip

If steps are chipped or stained, you can cover the top step and the treads with facing brick or create the appearance of bricks with a simple stenciling technique. Cut a couple of sponges in the shape of bricks (whole and half), dip them in brick-colored paint and stencil the steps in a running bond pattern where each row laps the next by half the length of the brick. Leave about a half-inch between bricks so the background cement looks like grout.

- Secure the stair railings and repaint them if necessary.
- Keep your street address numbers clearly visible and large enough for drive-by shoppers to see.

- Make certain your mailbox looks good and closes properly.
- Repair or replace any rundown fences or gates that might send a negative message about the entire property.

For Want of a Nail

One summer I was hired to help the owners of a hundred-year-old Victorian farmhouse figure out why their charming home wasn't selling. They'd rescued the house from near total disaster. The interior of the home was now perfection, and the exterior was beautiful.

Only one problem remained. They'd run out of money to redo the landscaping in the backyard, and decided to sell "as is."

The backyard had an uneven surface because the previous owner had filled the in-ground swimming pool with trash and old furniture. Any attempt to level the surface ultimately met with defeat, because as the furniture rotted, the ground continued to sink.

The owners were sure the problem was the uneven ground. I didn't think so. The ground didn't look like a golf course, but it was green.

The problem was the privacy fence. A number of boards had fallen from the fence, making it look a lot like an eight-year-old with missing teeth and a maniacal smile. Some of the posts were not straight and one whole section was completely missing. Well, not exactly missing, it was propped against the gate along with the loose boards, which, of course, meant the gate didn't work either.

I encouraged the young couple to repair the fence. Within twenty-four hours, the fence was repaired at a cost of $7.87 for nails and a new hinge. Within forty-eight hours, the house was sold to another young couple who had great plans for their private backyard.

One strong negative image can influence buyers' decisions. In other words, repair, replace, or remove anything that could reflect badly on your property.

Do whatever it takes—elbow grease, fresh paint, or even a new front door to create an inviting appearance. New brass hardware, a brass kick plate for the door, or new address numbers can add a lot of pizzazz without much expense. Use a sign of welcome such as a flowering wreath, a welcome mat, or a pot of flowers on the step to make a friendly first impression.

Stop Hedging Around

Most of the time I'm great at telling people exactly what they need to do to sell their homes, but once in a while, like most people, I take the easy way out.

When the agent told me that the listing I'd visited for him several weeks before hadn't sold, and he'd like me to go back, I had to admit that I knew what the problem was. I just hadn't had the heart to tell the owners.

They were an older couple who'd worked hard to get ready to sell, and they were justifiably proud of their home. They were doing okay, but neither of them was in the best of health.

The house was wonderful: spotless, and nicely decorated. There was only one real problem. The hedge next to the sidewalk was too high, too wide, and too long. It was neatly pruned, but extended over the sidewalk reducing the visibility to the front door and making passage to the house feel claustrophobic and uninviting. It also blocked the view to and from the picture window in the living room.

Unfortunately, the hedge was green only on the outside of the bushes; trimming it back wasn't an option. At the first meeting, I talked "around the edges" of relandscaping the walkway, but they were so unreceptive I chickened out rather than give them the bad news.

I'd really hoped the beautifully manicured yard and the wonderful interior would overcome the problem. But the agent said he couldn't even get people to come to the front door; they just drove up and drove away. This is often the problem when buyers can't see the front door. I went back to their home that day and gave that sweet, older couple the information they should have had when I'd visited them the first time. Happily, their unsuccessful weeks on the market made them far more receptive to my suggestions. The house sold right after they removed the hedge.

Everything else can be perfect, but if the outside space doesn't welcome buyers, you may lose the sale.

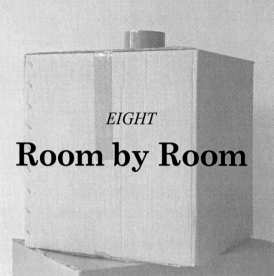

EIGHT

Room by Room

Now that you have addressed your outdoor space, it's time to move on to the interior spaces. Before you look at my room-specific suggestions, here are a few general guidelines that are true throughout your home.

General Guidelines

One—Make sure your home is clean and clutter-free.

Two—Keep big blocks of color neutral.

Three—Wash all windows.

Four—Leave shades up, drapes completely open, and blinds down, but open to permit the most available light to enter the room.

Five—Leave all lights on for showings, using the highest wattage light bulbs in each fixture throughout the home.

Six—Remove any unnecessary items such as wastebaskets, magazine piles, etc. to free as much floor space as possible and to create open traffic areas.

Seven—Remove all throw rugs!

Eight—Make sure pets are out of the house for showings and remove all signs of them as well —food dishes, litter boxes, toys, beds, etc.

Nine—Remove plants unless they are healthy, provide interest, and don't block the view from the windows.

Ten—Keep the quality high throughout your home with appropriate furnishings—i.e. don't use an outdoor trashcan in the kitchen, a lawn chair in the living room, or utility shelves anywhere except the basement, or garage.

Eleven—Conceal as many cords from lamps, appliances, TVs, and stereos as possible.

Twelve—Remove humidifiers, dehumidifiers, and portable space heaters to keep from creating unnecessary concerns.

I've chosen not to use a lot of pictures in this section so you won't get stuck trying to recreate a certain look but will find the best look for your home. Some of the suggestions are repeated to make it easier for you to tackle one space at a time without cross referencing.

As you work your way through the house, begin with the rooms your prospective buyers will see first and continue to use this approach throughout your home.

The Entry

Your entryway is vitally important. Unless there is a front porch, your entry is usually the first interior space a prospective buyer sees inside your home. The majority of people make their decision as soon as they walk in the door. They may not know if they are interested in buying, *but they know if they're not.* If the buyers don't like what they see right away, you might not get the opportunity to win them over with the rest of the house. Make their first view of your home as attractive as possible by:

- Storing all clothes trees, umbrella stands, large plants, and anything that may bump into your guests in this limited space.

- Removing any extra or off-season clothing and arranging the entry closet so it has some empty shelf, clothes rod, and floor space.

- Painting the entryway door and walls if they are not in good condition because they are seen up close and personal.

Quick Tip

A texturized or glazed finish can be a good choice in the entry because it can help hide the inevitable scuffs and nicks in this high-traffic area.

Then ensure a good first impression by:

- Testing the doorbell to make sure it works.

- Opening the curtains near your front door to invite people in.

- Leaving a lamp lit to make buyers feel welcome.

- Limiting color to accessories to keep from overwhelming buyers in close quarters.

- Using brass and glass accents to add some sparkle without color.

- Checking the view of the rest of your home from the entryway.

Quick Tip

Can buyers see an unmade bed, a desktop full of papers, or a sink full of dishes from the front entry? If the view extends through the house into the yard, buyers shouldn't see a clothesline full of laundry or a pile of compost either.

You can create a warm, friendly impression by engaging your buyers' senses with good lighting, fresh air, natural scents, and sweet sounds as soon as they enter your home. A pretty landscape or still life painting, a mirror, a bouquet of flowers, soft music, or the familiar scent of coffee, vanilla, or bread fresh from the oven can make the space more inviting.

Front and Back Porches

Like an entryway in the front of the house or a mudroom in the rear, a porch often forms the buyers' first and last impressions of a home. And although it's just fine to use a porch as a storage area or a playroom for small children, this is not advisable when your house is for sale.

When you're selling your home, you are marketing your home to the house-buying public, so it's important to use your porch to generate initial interest and enthusiasm for your property. Create an impression of a relaxing and leisurely lifestyle—just what everyone is looking for! Capture your buyers' attention by:

- Making sure the path from the porch door to the front door is unobstructed.
- Removing all toys, recyclables, old appliances, broken furniture, lawn and garden tools, etc. If the item wouldn't be a prop in an iced tea commercial or a cozy ski lodge—it needs to go.
- Putting away everything that does not bring peace and relaxation to mind.
- Cleaning the porch and porch windows thoroughly.
- Removing window coverings to welcome people in, rather than make them think they are intruding.
- Using *some* color to define the space to help people notice it.

> **Quick Tip**
> Create a summery effect with lots of white and a few splashes of color to give a fresh clean appearance. Accentuate various natural wood surfaces with some earth-toned accents or highlight an outdoorsy up-at-the-lake look with some color accents in forest green, burgundy, or navy blue.

You can complete the effect by:

- Arranging the furniture to accommodate both hobbies and relaxation such as a table and chairs for dining, playing cards, or working puzzles and a corner for watching TV, reading, or listening to your iPod.

- Creating a vignette to reveal the potential of the porch for various activities.

- Using lamp light in the evening, rather than the ceiling light common in most porches, to make the space appear more inviting.

Greet buyers with a wreath, a basket of flowers, a welcome sign, or anything else that says, *we're happy you've come to our home, come on in and sit a spell.*

Dining Room

The formal nature of dining rooms calls for a more traditional style. Whether they realize it or not, for most people, symmetrical design is part of what is expected in a traditional dining room. Symmetrical design means that furnishings and accessories in the room are placed so that if the room is divided in half visually, one half looks just like the other. A hutch pushed into the corner, a dining table placed against the wall, or an off-center lighting fixture can make buyers feel less comfortable. So increase your buyers' comfort level by:

- Creating balance at every opportunity.
- Centering the table.
- Using matching candleholders on the table or opposite sides of the buffet.
- Arranging glassware and plates symmetrically in the buffet.
- Centering any pictures or artwork on the available wall space.
- Focusing attention on your built-in buffet by not hanging art on the same wall.
- Removing any religious paintings.
- Turning the table in the direction that reduces congestion and facilitates traffic flow.
- Removing extra leaves from the dining table.
- Eliminating the captains' chairs and removing extra chairs.
- Removing colorful pads from your chairs.
- Placing chairs only on the ends or the sides of the table, rather than on all four sides if the dining room is small or narrow.
- Pushing the remaining dining room chairs as close to the table as possible.
- Adding a small table lamp to the buffet if the chandelier light is not sufficient.
- Polishing your dining furniture to add luster to the wood and reflective light to the space.
- Choosing only low centerpieces under a chandelier to keep from visually lowering the ceiling and pulling attention away from the light fixture.
- Leaving the chandelier lit to draw attention to it.
- Covering the table with a white or cream lace tablecloth or runner to add texture, light, and warmth to all the wood and solid surfaces.

- Giving potential buyers a reason to linger in your dining room by sparking their imagination with a vignette.

- Displaying your shiniest white, clear, or light-colored glassware and dishes in a glass-fronted hutch or buffet to reflect light.

- Using your built-in buffet to display information about your home such as dimensions, special features, financial info, and photos of the yard in other seasons to make sure potential buyers notice this selling feature.

I was once in a home where the owners used their built-in buffet to store all their paint cans and household cleaning and repair products. When I asked about it they told me that since they had no fancy crystal or tableware, this was very convenient. What do you think you would notice about the built-in buffet: leaded glass in the doors, or shelves loaded with paint cans?

Kitchen

The kitchen is considered one of the most important rooms in any home because many women make the decision to buy based on the condition and viability of the kitchen. Be sure to devote plenty of elbow grease and creativity to making it appear functional and look its best by:

- Greeting prospective buyers with something decorative, especially if the view from the front door includes the kitchen.

- Using the minimum number of kitchen chairs.

- Choosing chairs that fit close to the table.

- Keeping only one or two stools at snack counters.

- Setting a plate, silverware, mug or glass, and napkin on a place mat to emphasize a breakfast bar feature.

- Creating more floor space with a smaller kitchen table.

Improve the space even more by:

- Leaving most of the walls bare in small kitchens, especially if the room is wallpapered.

- Removing the dish rack, TV, coffeemaker, bread machine, and any other large items from the countertop.

- Freeing up crowded drawer space by putting wire whisks, spatulas, wooden spoons, and other utensils in a jar, inside the cupboard.

- Removing any unnecessary items from your cupboards and drawers.

- Arranging your cupboards and drawers to make your kitchen functional and convenient. For example, put your dinnerware in the cupboard nearest the table, sink or dishwasher; store pots and pans close to the stove; and place dishtowels near the sink.

- Grouping any remaining counter items away from the ends of the counters to prevent an accidental encounter.

- Eliminating pegboard, pot hooks, or racks that imply a lack of storage space.

- Keeping the pass-through from your kitchen to your dining or family room clutter-free.

- Giving your pass-through a bit of sparkle by placing a shiny tray and glassware on the counter between the rooms.

- Removing curtains from kitchen windows to add light and interest.

- Using a mirror that looks like a multi-pane window over the sink or on the wall in a window-less kitchen, to add light, dimension, and focus.

- Keeping windowsills and windows bare.

- Painting a small kitchen, doors, and trim with the same color cream or off-white paint, to unify the space.

- Updating old or unattractive cupboards with enamel paint and new hardware.

- Adding fresh appeal to color-dated appliances by having them electrostatically refinished.

- Storing any small appliances that don't complement your neutral palette.

- Creating a clutter and accident-free zone, by removing all magnets, calendars, and artwork from the refrigerator and cupboards.

- Removing pet food from the kitchen to eliminate turning off pet-less potential buyers.

- Packing away any extra coffee mugs or mug racks.

- Removing throw rugs to keep people from tripping or wondering if the rugs are covering worn spots.

- Using a diluted solution of bleach, liquid dish soap, and water to remove stains on white or very light-colored countertops, testing first to make sure the surface is colorfast.

- Removing all waste containers and recycling bins.

- Cleaning the grout around the sink with an old toothbrush and whitening toothpaste or bleach to capitalize on a great selling feature.

- Cleaning the oven and all burners on the stove.

- Making certain your kitchen smells fresh.

> ### Quick Tip
> If there's no time to clean, open the windows for a few minutes and then fill the sink with water and add a cleaning detergent like Mr. Clean or 409. Empty the sink before your buyers arrive to leave a fresh scent in the air for a long time.

- Replacing your burner pans with inexpensive aluminum ones if they're beyond help.

- Leaving each end of plate rails (1/4 of the length at each end) empty to keep from visually overwhelming buyers.

- Clearing everything except decorative items off the tops of cupboards and refrigerators.

- Using splashes of color in dishes, cookie jars, artwork, or other accessories to make your kitchen look its brightest and best.

Clean, clean, and CLEAN again!
You will NEVER get the best price
for your home if it's not CLEAN.

Living Room and Family Room

Depending on the type of home you have, your living room may or may not be the only leisure space in the house. These first ideas are applicable to all living and leisure spaces but are especially important the closer the main leisure space is to the beginning of the house tour. You can fashion a living space that quickly wins buyers over by:

- Keeping the entry area of the room open and inviting by removing any lamps, wall sconces, or furniture near the doorway.

- Creating a feeling of spaciousness by removing unnecessary furniture and leaving significant floor-to-ceiling breaks between conversational groupings.

> **Quick Tip**
>
> When you move furniture to a different location, you're often left with unsightly dents in the carpeting. You can make them far less noticeable by placing an ice cube on the indentation and letting it melt, then fluffing the area with a fork. Honest!

Make sure buyers see your living room at its best by:

- Placing your furniture so prospective buyers can easily walk through the room.

- Arranging your furnishings to draw attention to a focal point such as a fireplace or large window.

- Creating ambiance for showings with a fire in the fireplace, if weather permits.

- Removing or replacing any worn window coverings that could detract from the appearance of the room or the outside of the house.

- Opening the window coverings and moving lamps, plants, or pieces of furniture that block light from the windows.

- Limiting color to accessories as much as possible.

- Positioning TVs, entertainment centers, and computers so visitors do not see a tangle of cables and cords as they enter the room.

- Limiting the number of knickknacks and accessories on all surfaces.

- Using attractive, healthy plants to provide a touch of color and texture where you need it.

- Providing some interest and texture with a few knick-knacks such as books, magazines, plants, driftwood, unusual rocks, or baskets filled with candy, fruit, or nuts in the shell.

- Removing all but a few pieces of artwork in each room to allow buyers' eyes to rest and imagine their own artwork hanging there.

> **Quick Tip**
> Use artwork and paintings that complement the size of the wall. Hang your pictures at eye level, or about 6–12 inches above the sofa or chair that sits below your artwork. Leave one wall completely bare.

Living rooms often set the tone for the rest of the house. Make every effort to create a peaceful and organized environment if you want to put prospective buyers into a receptive mood.

Basement Recreation Rooms

These additional ideas are specifically chosen to make less-used rooms of the home seem accessible and attractive to potential buyers. While you may not be inclined to spend much time, effort, or money on these areas, I recommend you take a few minutes with this section. You may find that making just a couple of changes can improve the appearance of a room dramatically. In a market where you're competing for every advantage, this space could tip the scales. Make your recreation rooms look more inviting by:

- Increasing bulb wattage or purchasing an extra lamp or two.

- Replacing dated and shabby lampshades to update the room's decor and provide both visual and lighting impact.

- Using light colors in rooms with less natural light to brighten up the space.

- Keeping these rooms clean to indicate to potential buyers that you use these spaces.

- Reviving any worn upholstered furniture with a slipcover or throw in a neutral color.

- Anchoring a conversational grouping and covering unattractive floors with an area rug to make a space feel cozier.

- Tossing a few coordinating pillows on the sofa and chairs to provide a unifying element and give your room a more pulled-together look.

- Hanging a couple of coordinating posters in inexpensive poster frames to give focus and interest.

It's very important to let buyers know your recreation room is a valuable living space and frequently used by your family. Reinforce this message with a current magazine, newspaper, or open book on a chair or coffee table. You might even add a mug of coffee or a can of soda nearby.

Bedrooms

Because of the intimate nature of bedrooms, it is especially important to make people feel comfortable in this personal space. You can make your bedrooms more attractive to buyers by:

- Keeping furnishings to an absolute minimum in small bedrooms.

- Arranging furniture to make the most of available floor space and facilitate traffic flow.

- Using the largest size bed you have available, without crowding the space, so buyers don't have to guess what size bed the room can accommodate.

- Positioning the dressers and chests as far away from the bedroom door as you can to make them appear smaller.

- Placing a bedroom dresser with a mirror across from the room's doorway to make the space seem larger.

- Avoiding the placement of the bed under a window unless you have no other choice—it signals inadequate wall space.

- Using a plain bed frame to give visitors more walking space.

- Keeping lamps in proportion to the nightstands, chests, and dressers and placing them as far from the entryway as possible.

- Removing clutter from the dresser, chest, and tabletops.

- Replacing any stained, faded, or worn carpet, or removing it and leaving the floors bare.

- Keeping closets partially empty to indicate adequate storage.

- Eliminating portable TVs, especially if they sit near the entry area of the bedroom.

- Keeping hooks, pegs, racks, and chairs free from clothing.

- Covering your bedroom windows with clean, functional window shades or blinds to give buyers a feeling of privacy.

- Limiting the bedroom colors to an understated palette to create relaxed and ready buyers.

> **Quick Tip**
> Many people like softer shades of blue and green in bedrooms because they are calming and conducive to peace and relaxation—some say they even lower blood pressure. If you really want some color, painting a bedroom in these colors is a good choice.

You can create the most appealing look by:

- Using neutrally colored sheers on your windows, to allow light but filter problems if the view or the condition of your woodwork could be a detriment to a sale.

- Placing one pillow on a twin bed, two on a full, three on a queen, and four on a king so people can easily determine what size bed is in the room.

Quick Tip

Rather than propping pillows up so they stand on edge, lay them down. Although it is less fashionable, it gives the room a longer sight line, making it seem larger.

Horizontal lines are more soothing than vertical lines. Use them in your blinds, shades, curtains, bed linens, or artwork to create a more restful space. Remember: comfortable, relaxed buyers are more likely to buy your home.

Master Bedrooms

Many homes today have master bedroom suites. Along with following the suggestions for bedrooms, if you have any extra room in the master bedroom, create a *suite* effect by:

- Using flattering lamp light to create an inviting, relaxing, and romantic mood.

- Conjuring up visions of quiet leisure time with a small round skirted table and easy chair, complete with teapot, mug, and a good book all nestled in a cozy nook.

- Making the bedroom look inviting with a pretty throw pillow, a simple rose on the bed, a vase of flowers, and a couple candles.

- Creating a home office corner with a desk, lamp, and chair.

- Appealing to the workout enthusiast with an arrangement of sports equipment.

Make certain the master bedroom is neat, clean, and inviting even if the other bedrooms don't get much attention. After all, the master bedroom is the buyer's bedroom.

Kids' Bedrooms

Kids' rooms are often decorated to appeal to a very specific age and gender child. You can expand the potential of a child's bedroom by:

- Eliminating as many toys, stuffed animals, or dolls on beds, chairs, and shelves as possible.

- Using generic bedroom lamps (without a theme).

- Reducing the impact of color by taking out anything that can easily be removed such as posters, sports, hobby or cartoon accessories, glow-in-the-dark stick-ons, pillows, mobiles, or rugs, etc.

- Removing as much child-specific decor as possible to appeal to a larger age range.

As a general rule, eliminate as many of the non-essentials as you can without ruining the parent/child relationship.

Spare Rooms

It's normally fine to use a spare room as storage, but when your house is for sale, you want prospective buyers to see all the living space available to them. Therefore, don't use a spare room for storage unless absolutely necessary, and never if the spare room is on the main floor, where it is one of the first rooms your buyers see upon entering your house. If there isn't an extra bed available, making a home office or an exercise room out of a spare bedroom works just as well. In either case, make it look its best by:

- Placing furniture away from the doorway to prevent narrowing the entry area.

- Clearing as much floor space as possible.

- Keeping furnishings to a minimum.

- Positioning your monitor, printer, etc. as far away from the doorway as you can.

- Leaving the window coverings open to add natural light.

- Painting the walls with neutral colors.

Keep distractions at a minimum by:

- Hiding all cords and cables, especially those near the doorway.

- Keeping desktop surfaces free of piles of paper or books.

You can also set the stage for a workout space with a chair with a towel on it, a jump rope, a set of small dumb bells, or a mirror on the wall.

It's fine to leave a spare room empty as long as it has been well-maintained. However, with nothing else to look at, any imperfections on the ceiling, walls, or floor are more noticeable, and brightly painted walls can overwhelm the buyer. You'll need to keep the colors neutral and the room in pristine condition if it is left bare.

Bathrooms

The top priority in the bathroom is to make things look as impersonal, clean, and spacious as possible. The bathroom area is a very personal place, and people feel more comfortable when the owner's presence is less evident. You can make your bathroom look its best by:

- Keeping all personal products out of sight and making sure any shelves are partially empty.

- Opening your shower curtain or sliding door all the way against the wall farthest away from the door to make the bathroom feel larger and show off any ceramic tile in the tub and shower area.

- Removing the shower curtain valance to give the area a cleaner line and make the room feel larger.

- Eliminating towels on shower door towel bars will make the bathroom seem wider.

- Putting away your wastebasket, rug, scale, kiddie stool, or anything else that reduces the available floor space.

- Removing curtains and replacing them with space-saving mini-blinds or translucent contact paper on window glass in small bathrooms.

- Leaving the lights on in bathrooms prevents potential buyers from having to search for hard-to-find lights located under the towels on the towel bar, attached to the light fixture, or behind the door.

- Reducing color in the bathroom with cream or white towels, tissue boxes, toilet paper, and soap to make the room feel more sanitary, less personal, and larger.

- Replacing your current shower curtain with an inexpensive cream, white, or clear curtain or liner to reduce the impact of color in the bathroom.

- Using light colors in the bathroom to make it look lighter, brighter, bigger, and cleaner.

You can make potential buyers feel more comfortable in this personal space by:

- Removing everything from the vanity top, the back of the toilet, the window sill, the edges of the bathtub, the floor, and the back of the door.

- Arranging the contents of the medicine cabinet and the linen closet, so nothing will fall out if it is opened.

- Removing toilet tank covers and seat covers to show condition of the water closet and reduce color.

- Cleaning or re-grouting ceramic tile to add value to this selling feature.

- Laying a new line of caulk around the tub and sink to crisply detail your bathroom.

- Keeping any plungers, toilet brushes, or other plumbing equipment out of sight.

- Removing and replacing or repainting any discolored bathroom fans or heating vents.

- Opening the windows or turning on a fan to air out the bathroom.

- Replacing any damp towels or bathmats with clean, fluffy, new ones.

- Keeping bathrooms from feeling uncomfortably personal and humid by bathing several hours before a showing.

- Removing your portable space heater to keep buyers from thinking your heating system is inadequate.

- Using only scent-free air neutralizers to eliminate odors without adding any additional fragrance.

- Bringing out the elbow grease to make the bathroom shine, shine, shine.

Now that the clutter has been removed, the space depersonalized, and the shine restored, return interest with a couple accessories. Some luxury bath items, a pretty soap dish and glass, a small fountain, a vase of flowers, or a vignette can help make this room more attractive and less personal—more *fun*—less *fun*ction.

Unfinished Basement or Attic Space

An unfinished basement or attic is just that—unfinished. Therefore, your goal is to help a buyer to recognize the room's potential and to help them get a clear view of the space. Increase your basement or attic potential by:

- Moving everything as far away from the basement steps as you can to help buyers easily see the space.

- Keeping the basement steps safe, well-lit, and unobstructed.

- Buying self-adhesive stair treads for painted basement steps to keep a sale from *slipping* away.

- Making the basement appear larger by placing something in a far corner to create a longer view with a diagonal sight line.

- Using the highest wattage bulbs in each fixture to make the area brighter.

- Cleaning thoroughly to get rid of spider webs and dust.

- Painting all the walls white to make your basement look clean, feel fresh, and smell like new construction—just waiting for new owners to make it into something special.

- Removing debris and leaves from window wells to let in more light and make your home look well-maintained.

- Washing all basement windows to let in the most possible light.

- Stacking all boxes and possessions neatly, in the least noticeable corner of the room.

Unfinished space can be an asset not a liability. Most basements are not finished the way new owners might choose, so unfinished space gives potential buyers a way to realize their own dreams.

Laundry Room

Your laundry room can be a key area when selling your home. Even if the basement is not used for anything else, most homeowners use their washers and dryers on a weekly basis, and many people use the laundry daily, so it should be clean, brightly lit, and a bit colorful.

Surprised? Most of us associate clean laundry with the images we've seen on laundry soap packaging and commercials. These commercials and products are a riot of color; therefore, your laundry room is one place where color works well. When staging your laundry area, make it resemble a laundry commercial as much as possible by:

- Cleaning the entire area to rid the laundry room of lint puffs from the dryer, and any unwanted guests.
- Removing shabby curtains.
- Eliminating or containing any dirty laundry.
- Raising clotheslines high and keeping them taut, empty, and out of the way.
- Putting a folding table between your washer and dryer to create a more unified space if the appliances are not situated close to each other.
- Buying an inexpensive florescent shop light for a laundry room with inadequate light.
- Placing a throw rug in front of the laundry tubs or washer and dryer to define the space and make it feel cleaner.

Quick Tip
Brightly colored pastel rugs with white stripes help bring the idea of fresh clean laundry to mind but any clean, fresh-looking rug will do.

- Avoiding doing wash before buyers come to keep the laundry area from feeling damp and clammy.

Put on the finishing touches by:

- Arranging all your laundry supplies face forward to show off their colorful packaging.

- Piling a stack of freshly laundered and neatly folded towels (colorful beach towels work well) on the dryer, to add to the clean laundry feeling.
- Placing a small flowering plant on the windowsill to make things look fresh and cheerful.
- Airing out the laundry room so it smells fresh and clean too.

Your goal is to make it seem like doing the laundry would make your buyers feel as fresh as a mountain spring, a field of flowers or, at the very least, that doing the wash wouldn't be as much of a chore in this pleasant space.

Furnace Room

When unfinished and maintenance areas of the home, such as the basement, furnace room, laundry area, attic, etc., are clean and well-tended, it sends a strong, positive message to buyers about the condition of your home. You can add to your buyers' comfort level by:

- Keeping the access to the furnace area as obstacle-free as possible.
- Making sure the area is well-lit so potential buyers can examine the furnace, water heater, and other appliances.
- Dusting the furnace, water heater, air conditioner, water softener, and your other appliances so buyers will assume they have been well cared-for and are in good condition.
- Painting walls with light-colored paint.
- Vacuuming the furnace and surrounding area.
- Cleaning the furnace room thoroughly. Cleaning the furnace room may seem unimportant, but "The sale is in the details."

- Placing the owner's manuals for your furnace, etc. in clear plastic folders and attaching them to the appliances to assure buyers your home has received regular maintenance and loving care.

When the least visible areas of the home are a high priority, new buyers feel comfortable that there are no unseen repairs ahead—an important consideration for today's buyers.

Garage

Garages are similar to basements and attics, in that most people use them for storage; therefore, the same rules apply. Impress potential buyers with your organizational detail by:

- Cleaning out the garage.
- Keeping garage partially empty.
- Storing essentials at the back of the garage, leaving the sides completely free of clutter, to make the space look larger.
- Renting a storage unit or buying a shed to house the things that are cluttering the space.
- Washing any windows to increase the natural light.
- Disposing of anything you are not moving with you.
- Keeping storage all in one place—as far from view as possible.
- Arranging the garage so that two cars will fit in a two-car garage and so on.
- Parking only one car in a two-car garage during showings, making sure it takes up less than half the area so it is easier for prospective buyers to evaluate the space.

You'll get extra points with buyers if it appears you haven't yet exhausted all your property's storage areas and have plenty of room for all their stuff.

Decks

Decks are similar to porches, and the advice about porches is certainly true of decks. Like porches, decks are meant for relaxation and should be furnished to evoke leisure not labor.

Do whatever you can to help buyers visualize outdoor living in their new home. Be sure to enhance this "outdoor room" if you want to improve your sales prospects. *Do not leave the deck empty.* If furnished, a deck registers as another room—an outdoor room. If left empty, the space may not register at all. Stack the deck by furnishing it with:

- a picnic table,
- a grill,
- lawn chairs, or a chaise lounge,
- a small table that holds a can of soda, some sunscreen, an open magazine,
- and for color—pots of flowers in the summer and pots of evergreens in the winter.

Quick Tip

If you live in a townhouse or condo, check the regulations to see if grills are permitted on the decks in your development.

Make sure the placement of your grill, deck furniture, etc. does not block the sun or the view from inside your home. For example, at my house, if the two Adirondack chairs we use on the deck are placed in front of the picture window, it spoils the view of the creek from the living room.

The Backyard

Even though the backyard is the last area to be covered, it still remains an extremely important part of the selling strategy because it is often the last area potential buyers see before they leave.

If you must leave some things out, gather them neatly together, making sure that the corner you choose to put them in is the one that is the least noticeable. Make your backyard one that closes the deal by:

- Eliminating all piles of everything including logs, wood chips, landscaping supplies, paving stones, or sand for the Zen garden you haven't gotten around to creating yet.
- Removing anything that isn't decorative.
- Avoiding attracting attention to your neighbors' shortcomings.

This is a good place for a little sleight of hand. If your neighbors have a rundown dog house next to your fence, then put a bird feeder on the other side of the yard to attract attention away from the eyesore. If the side of their home facing yours has peeling paint or a pile of junk, plant something in that area of your property—shrubs, trees, vines, etc. to help keep the buyers' attention on your property, not your neighbor's.

NINE

Vignettes:
Settings That Sell

Now that you've used space, light, and color to your advantage and your home is clean, orderly, and attractive, it's time for vignettes—the finishing touches that set the stage for a sale.

The dictionary says vignettes "embellish, enhance, illuminate, and dress to advantage." In decorating terms, vignettes are small scenes that create a focus, set a mood, and describe something in a brief but elegant way.

Vignettes give the potential buyer reason to linger in a room and use their imagination to glimpse the good life that can be theirs if they purchase your home. They can be especially valuable in rooms that need a focal point or are lacking interest.

As the seller, the feeling you want to foster in a buyer is comfort, happiness, and stress-free living. Vignettes can be a way to reinforce this response in the buyer.

Porch or Deck

On a porch or deck you want to evoke a feeling of leisure, so:

- Place an afghan on a chair or chaise with an open book.

- Set out a glass of iced tea with the newspaper and a pair of sunglasses.

- Put some bedding plants on a table with gardening tools and gloves.

- Place a beach towel, sunscreen, and magazine on a lounge chair on your deck.

Living Room

In a living room or family room you might:

- Set up a puzzle, a board game, or a hand of solitaire.

- Arrange a game of darts, pool, pingpong, or pinball, so it looks as if you are in the middle of a game.

- Place a bowl of popcorn, a video, and a couple cans of soda on a coffee table.

- Set the stage for happy memories with roasting sticks, marshmallows, graham crackers, and chocolate bars in a room with a fireplace.

- Use a blanket, picnic basket, and a bottle of wine with a couple wine glasses to suggest the idea of a romantic, fireside picnic.

- Tuck a coffee mug and a book in a cozy reading corner.

Bedroom

In a bedroom you might:

- Place a folded napkin, a cup of tea, a croissant, a folded newspaper, and a flower on a bed tray to give the room a lazy Sunday feeling.

- Lay a single rose (silk won't wilt) and an envelope on the bed or pillow.

- Put an old photo, a lace handkerchief, and a piece of old costume jewelry on the bed or dresser.

Dining Room

In a dining room you might:

- Place a couple of wine glasses on the dining table or buffet with a bouquet of flowers or a small wrapped package.

- Set the table for an intimate dinner for two using linen napkins, lace tablecloth, pretty china, teapot, chopsticks, fondue pot, covered tureen, flowers, candles—anything that speaks of special times.

Bathroom

In a bathroom you could create a soothing atmosphere by using a few small luxuries such as:

- bath beads,

- a pretty candle,

- a package of incense,

- a potpourri pot,

- a bottle of Perrier and a pretty glass,

- a fancy soap,

- a small bunch of lavender,

- a bottle of bath oil or lotion—anything that says comfort and relaxation to you.

Place your choices in a basket, with a big, fluffy bath towel and other spa essentials and just try to resist.

Workshop

In a workshop, you could:

- Arrange a ruler, a project plan or blueprint, a coffee mug, and a pad of paper with a materials list on a workbench or table.

- Create the impression of a work in progress, with a plain wooden birdhouse, paints, and a brush.

Backyard

In the backyard, to capitalize on recreational possibilities you might:

- Place a pitcher of lemonade and a couple of glasses on the picnic table.

- Put the ingredients for s'mores on your grill.

- Arrange a basket with garden gloves, scissors, and fresh-cut flowers near a flower bed. To keep the flowers fresh, wrap the stems in wet paper towels and a plastic bag and cover them with the garden gloves or a bandana.

- Set up a game of croquet in the back yard.

- Hang a hammock (complete with book) between two trees.

Don't go overboard with vignettes, one or two will do nicely. Keep your eyes open for any arrangement of objects that can create a point of interest. You can find vignette ideas on nearly every page in magazines, including the advertisements.

Even though vignettes may seem a bit contrived, I know they make a difference. When my own home was for sale, I tried an experiment. I set out a basket of grapes and two jars of grape jelly (one for the agent and one for the buyers) for some of the showings. I included a note saying the jelly was a thank you for visiting our home and that it was made from the grapes on the fence in our backyard—which was true.

I set the jars out for only three of the eighteen showings. The first time I created the vignette, the potential buyers didn't take the jelly, which told me they were not interested. The next time the buyers took it, returned for a second showing, but decided against buying the house. The third couple took the jelly and bought the house. They offered us full price for the house and $5,000 more, even though there were no competing bids.

Before we closed, the buyers asked if they could come over so we could show them how to care for their new home. When they came, we were greeted with hugs and pastries. I can't help but think that it was the jar of jelly that started the relationship off on such a sweet note!

TEN

Staging a Vacant House

Even when the homes are empty, builders have no trouble selling new construction. So why is it so difficult to sell existing houses when they're vacant? What's the difference?

The difference between a new home and a vacant house is the buyer's perception, expectations, and comfort level.

New Construction	Vacant House
• The buyers' perception of new construction is that it is new, clean, and ready for immediate occupancy.	• The buyers' perception of a vacant house is that it is used, dirty, needs work, and takes time.
• The question buyers ask about new construction is "Can we afford it?"	• The question buyers ask about a vacant house is "Why is it empty?"
• Their expectation is that it is in perfect condition.	• Their expectation is that it is in questionable condition.
• *The focus is on the future.*	• *The focus is on the past.*

In a word, everything about new construction says *desirable* and everything about a vacant house says *undesirable*.

The buyers' perception of a house, along with their expectations, equals their comfort level. Buyers have a high degree of comfort in new construction and a much lower level of comfort in vacant houses.

In order to sell your vacant house, it's necessary to level the playing field—to make buyers feel as comfortable about your vacant house as they feel about new construction. You can make buyers feel more comfortable in your vacant house by:

- Leaving the heat on in the winter and the air conditioning on in the summer. Set the thermostat comfortably at seventy degrees. Buyers want to live in comfortable homes, not meat lockers or ovens.

- Turning lights on, both inside and outside. If agents can't see to open the lock box, they can't show the house. Use timers to reduce electricity costs, but make certain the lights are on for showings— focus on warm, inviting, low-level lighting.

- Leaving a radio playing on a classical music station. Just make sure the dial's not set on a talk radio station. Hearing an unexpected voice in an empty house could spook a seller.

- Providing a place for buyers to sit and discuss a purchase agreement. A couple of stools at the kitchen counter or a table and chairs in a well-lit spot are absolutely essential. The more comfortable they are, the longer they stay. The longer they stay, the more likely they are to make an offer.

Even if you decide not to make any other changes, these four suggestions alone will increase potential buyers' physical and psychological comfort. Many scary movies take place in a cold, dark, silent, and empty house. Your buyers have seen those movies too.

However, it's not enough to keep from scaring people away. With little to distract them, potential buyers see every speck of dirt, every smudged and streaky window, every flaw in the paint, the floors and the ceilings. In essence, there is a much higher standard of cleanliness and maintenance expected of vacant properties if they are to compete with their new construction counterparts. You can rise to this higher level of expectations by:

- Making sure all walls, floors, rugs, and ceilings are in pristine condition.
- Cleaning regularly.
- Washing windows.
- Keeping up the yard work in the summer.
- Shoveling, snowblowing, and salting driveways and sidewalks to keep them free of ice in the winter.
- Airing out the house frequently.

Even though many stagers bring in furnishings, I don't believe it's necessary to fill your vacant home with furniture. Time and again, I've seen homeowners spend a lot of money renting furnishings to make their empty house look occupied. However, with very few exceptions the furniture doesn't look "at home". In fact, most of the time, it looks lonely. You just can't put a straight chair in the corner of the bedroom with a floor lamp and call it furnished.

I think it's much more effective to stage the areas where a little magic goes a long way. First, maximize the best features of your home. For example, if you have a fireplace, hang a picture over it and put a couple shiny things on the mantel. If you have a beautiful view, place a bird house or some statuary outside to draw attention out the window—remember to use red to help buyers notice details.

Second, accessorize any lonely furniture. Even a lone chair and lamp in a corner can look more inviting if you place a small table next to it with a magazine and coffee mug or can of soda.

Third, use vignettes. The entryway, dining room, kitchen, bath, and laundry are all rooms that don't require furniture to make the space look homey. By putting together vignettes in these areas, you create opportunities for guests to linger. You can also offer some inviting details such as:

- A basket of booties by the entry door so buyers feel a little pampered—and so do your floors.

- A bowl of candy on the kitchen counter.

- A refrigerator stocked with beverages and a note on the counter telling buyers to help themselves.

- A pad of notepaper and a pen.

By adding accessories to lonely furniture, highlighting features, and creating vignettes, you can dispel the impression that the house has been abandoned and put the focus on the future. Little touches such as a pasta bowl, an attractive bottle of olive oil, a wooden spoon, bag of pasta, and a recipe book on the counter in the kitchen, show an attention to detail that says: *Welcome, this is a wonderful home, we love it, and we've prepared it—just for you.*

ELEVEN

Photographing Your Home for Marketing on the Internet

As I mentioned previously, nearly 90 percent of all home buyers find their homes on the Internet before they visit them in person. While you may have *dozens* of people drive by your home and notice it's for sale, on-line viewers number in the *thousands*. Consequently, without good photos, you greatly limit your opportunity to sell your home.

Creating eye-catching photos that look attractive when they pop up together collage-style in such a small format, presents a unique challenge to the photographer. Without careful planning, the pictures can appear too busy to sort out easily and cause buyers to click right past your home.

Here are several tricks to help you get the best possible photos of your home.

- Like people, most homes look better from one side or the other. View your house from the street to determine whether your home's profile is more interesting from the right or left side.

- Photograph your home from an angle, instead of straight on, to give it more dimension, interest, and the longest possible sightline.

- Make certain the sun is behind you so the picture is not distorted by shadows.

- Be sure to take your window reflections into consideration. Besides creating shadows, light can also reflect on your windows and either add to the beauty of your home or detract from it.

- Take photos at different times of the day to find the light that most flatters your home. You might want to try taking your pictures later in the day. The color of the light at sunset can give a beautiful quality to outdoor photos and the lower angle of the sun helps to eliminate reflections.

- Capture your address numbers in the picture if possible.

Use these suggestions when taking photos of the inside of your home:

- Take your pictures with all the lights on.

- Rotate your lamp shades so the seams are out of sight.

- Keep the largest furniture as far away as possible so perspective will work for you.

- Minimize patterns in your photos. Obvious prints and patterns tend to look busy in small Internet photos.

- Leave sufficient empty wall space so the rooms don't appear crowded.

- Use fewer accessories than usual since less looks like *more* in pictures.

- Make sure there is nothing in the forefront of the photo to block the view through the room.

- Take your pictures from the longest sightline to make the room appear more spacious.

- Do not aim your camera directly at the window. If you want to highlight the windows, take the photo from an angle.

- Center your pictures on the focal point or best asset of the room. For example, a fireplace would be considered an obvious focal point in a living room. However, the best feature in a kitchen might be beautiful cabinets or a window over the sink. In a room without interesting details, create your own focal point with decorative accessories or a vignette.

- Keep your rooms simple and uncluttered to make them look their best when they appear together on a small computer screen.

- Like your exterior photos, you may need to take the interior pictures on both cloudy and sunny days and at different times to catch the most becoming light.

Select the photos that showcase your home's best features. For example, it's more important to choose a photo with the best view of your living room fireplace than it is to include every piece of furniture in the room. And it's better to give buyers an overall impression of your landscaping than it is to focus on your award-winning dahlias.

Buyers that schedule a showing based on the photos you've presented are already partially sold. So, if you show them the house they're already interested in, looking its best—you're likely to sell them the rest of the way.

A home that *meets* expectations
is a GOOD DEAL,
but a home that *exceeds* expectations
is a STEAL!

Parting Thoughts

Throughout my years helping people prepare to sell their homes quickly and profitably, many clients say they find their homes much more attractive after my visit. They often tell me if I had come sooner they might have chosen not to move. Luckily for me, many of them invite me to come to their new homes as well. They think the secret lies in me and my magic. However, I'm convinced the process is really not magic at all, but skills that are easily learned.

Now that you've read what I have to say about staging your home and have acquired your own staging skills, I'd like to hear what you have to say. I'd be delighted if you would e-mail me at Diane@DianeKeyes.com with your own *This Sold House* success story. I love to hear good news!

I sincerely hope *This Sold House* is as fun for you to read and use as it has been for me to live and write. Whether you're moving in or out, I encourage you to make changes that will add to your enjoyment of your home as long as you live there—and increase your profits when you sell, making both your bank account and your spirit soar.

Diane Keyes

About the Author

One of the first staging professionals, **Diane Keyes** has been bringing her innovative approach to the real estate industry for more than twenty years.

Her unique talents have brought her to four-star restaurants, multi-million-dollar island get-aways, and thousands of private homes. And when they needed someone to prepare the state mansion for the Swedish royal family the governor's wife called Diane.

She first began teaching classes in 1988 and has since taught her staging methods to many realtors seeking to fulfill their continuing education requirements.

Along with consummate staging advice, Diane brings understanding and insight to the complex psychological issues surrounding the sale of a home, a much ignored but vitally important facet of real estate sales.

Her book, *Spirit of the Snowpeople*, will soon be released by DownEast Books. With several books in the works, and her poetry being performed at the Center for the Arts in Bloomington Minnesota for the past three years, she is not only a pioneer in the staging industry, but an accomplished author as well. Writing *This Sold House* was a natural step for Diane as she continues to find better ways to help homeowners sell their homes in the changing marketplace.

Diane lives in Minneapolis, Minnesota with her husband Tom. She has two married children and one perfect grandchild.

Would You Like More?

Complete the form below or order at www.thissoldhouse.biz/order

Feel free to copy this page to make ordering easier.

Book Request

❑ Please send me additional copies of *This Sold House.*

___ copies at $14.95 per copy	_____
MN sales tax 6.5%	_____
Shipping in North America	$5.95
Shipping abroad	+ $12.95
TOTAL	_____

Shipping Information

Name_____

Street Address _____

City _____

State_____   Zip _____

❑ Please keep my name and address confidential.

Payment Information

❑ Visa   ❑ MasterCard

Number _____   Exp. Date _____

Mail this form to:

This Sold House

P.O. 32092

Minneapolis, MN 55432

Questions?

E-mail Diane Keyes at *diane@thissoldhouse.biz*